WALLS FALL DOWN

7 STEPS *from the* BATTLE OF JERICHO TO OVERCOME ANY CHALLENGE

DUDLEY RUTHERFORD

NELSON
BOOKS

An Imprint of Thomas Nelson

Published in Nashville, Tennessee, by Thomas Nelson. Thomas Nelson is a registered trademark of Thomas Nelson, Inc.

Published in association with Alive Communications, 7680 Goddard Street, Suite 200, Colorado Springs, CO 80920.

Thomas Nelson, Inc., titles may be purchased in bulk for educational, business, fundraising, or sales promotional use. For information, please e-mail SpecialMarkets@ ThomasNelson.com.

Cataloging-in-Publication Data available through the Library of Congress

978-1-4002-0603-2

Printed in the United States of America

14 15 16 17 18 RRD 6 5 4 3 2 1

This book about the walls of Jericho falling down is dedicated to my father, H. Dean Rutherford, who for more than half a century made Bible stories jump off the page in dramatic fashion. May this book be an extension of his imaginative storytelling ability and leave an indelible mark on the hearts and minds of every reader.

CONTENTS

CONTENTS

Now the gates of Jericho were securely barred because of the Israelites. No one went out and no one came in.

Then the LORD said to Joshua, "See, I have delivered Jericho into your hands, along with its king and its fighting men. March around the city once with all the armed men. Do this for six days. Have seven priests carry trumpets of rams' horns in front of the ark. On the seventh day, march around the city seven times, with the priests blowing the trumpets. When you hear them sound a long blast on the trumpets, have the whole army give a loud shout; then the wall of the city will collapse and the army will go up, everyone straight in."

So Joshua son of Nun called the priests and said to them, "Take up the ark of the covenant of the LORD and have seven priests carry trumpets in front of it." And he ordered the army, "Advance! March around the city, with an armed guard going ahead of the ark of the LORD."

When Joshua had spoken to the people, the seven priests carrying the seven trumpets before the LORD went forward, blowing their trumpets, and the ark of the LORD's covenant followed them. The armed guard marched ahead of the priests who blew the trumpets, and the rear guard followed the ark. All this time the trumpets were sounding. But Joshua had commanded the army, "Do not give a war cry, do not raise your voices, do not say a word until the day I tell you to shout. Then shout!" So he had the ark of the LORD carried around the city, circling it once. Then the army returned to camp and spent the night there.

Joshua got up early the next morning and the priests took up the ark of the LORD. The seven priests carrying the seven trumpets went forward, marching before the ark of the LORD and blowing the trumpets. The armed men went ahead of them and the rear guard followed the ark of the LORD, while the trumpets kept sounding. So on the second day they marched around the city once and returned to the camp. They did this for six days.

On the seventh day, they got up at daybreak and marched around the city seven times in the same manner, except that on that day they circled the city seven times. The seventh time around, when the priests sounded the trumpet blast, Joshua commanded the army, "Shout! For the LORD has given you the city! The city and all that is in it are to be devoted to the LORD. Only Rahab the prostitute and all who are with her in her house shall be spared, because she hid the spies we sent. But keep away from the devoted things, so that you will not bring about your own destruction by taking any of them. Otherwise you will make the camp of Israel liable to destruction and bring trouble on it. All the silver and gold and the articles of bronze and iron are sacred to the LORD and must go into his treasury."

When the trumpets sounded, the army shouted, and at the sound of the trumpet, when the men gave a loud shout, the wall collapsed; so everyone charged straight in, and they took the city.

JOSHUA 6:1–20

INTRODUCTION

SETTING THE STAGE

I t has all the essential ingredients of an epic movie or novel. A hero from humble beginnings leads a group of courageous and loyal men to conquer a city whose inhabitants are, by all accounts, more numerous and muscular than they are. Massive fortified walls—impenetrable by human force—encompass the prized city. Yet, with divine guidance, they prepare for battle, advance on the city, and *win*.

But this is no fictional tale. This is a historical victory that occurred nearly four thousand years ago when an ordinary man by the name of Joshua led an army of faithful soldiers to conquer the city of Jericho in a land God had promised to the Israelites.[1] The odds were not just stacked against Joshua and his army—there were no odds, for the inhabitants of Jericho were bigger, stronger, and more powerful than the people of Israel (Num. 13:26–33). However, God imparted to Joshua an unconventional plan of attack, which led to a famed victory over this formidable city.

Because Joshua and the Israelites had the courage to set aside their human wisdom and efforts and follow God's specific and unusual instructions, they were able to achieve an awe-inspiring military upset that is still being talked about today.

Countless battles have been waged throughout the ages, and most of the particulars of these historical skirmishes have long since been forgotten. But the details of this battle and this victory remain vivid and distinguished. No city has ever been defeated in the surprising manner in which Jericho fell so long ago.

WHAT IS YOUR JERICHO?

Buried deep within this ancient story are principles of success that we can use today. In reading God's instructions to Joshua before the Battle of Jericho, I discovered seven spiritual strategies that have the power to help you conquer any contemporary foe. I truly believe that if you follow and apply these steps diligently—just as Joshua and the Israelites did—any obstacle, trial, or problem you are facing will crumble at your feet.

And I don't make this claim lightly.

Many of us read big promises with a bit of healthy skepticism because we have stood in the midst of a battle that seemed unwinnable. Even when we make strides toward a better future, we're invariably met with overwhelming walls or obstacles that block our progress. And along comes a book with a catchy little title, and we think, *I'll give it a try because nothing else has worked.*

Whether our battles are related to our finances, careers, health, or relationships, we strive to overcome them. Embedded in our DNA is a desire for victory and a capacity to dream of what life could be if only things went our way. But the harsh reality is that there are certain seasons of life that simply become a daily grind of difficult trials.

How many people do you know who are sinking under the weight of debt or an addiction to drugs or alcohol? How many people are struggling in their marriages and families or are going through a divorce? How many are in bondage to pornography, eating disorders, or gambling? Can you think of even one person in your life who is *not* struggling in some area or another? Some of these might sound familiar:

- The newly wedded couple dreams of marital bliss, only to discover a long road of conflict and troubles. They give up hope and trudge over to the nearest divorce attorney but realize that this is just the beginning of real heartache and headache.
- A soldier heads to war in hopes that he will return to his family unscathed. But after surviving an enemy blast, he returns home with debilitating physical injuries as well as deep emotional scars from the atrocities he witnessed in combat.
- Parents, whose children seemed so sweet and innocent such a short time ago, now anguish and pray and worry for their teenage sons and daughters who are caught up in drugs, gangs, cutting, eating disorders, depression, sex, or unscrupulous friends.
- An elderly couple on the verge of retirement, having worked tirelessly for forty years and pinched every penny, watches as the failure of the financial institutions wipes out their life savings.

- A young woman, after a night of passion, wakes up the next morning regretting her decision to be intimate and commits never to give in again, but gets the result from the little test that she's pregnant—or worse, HIV positive—and her life will never be the same.

There are countless others who have hit a wall in their spiritual lives. Jesus declared in John 10:10 that He came into the world so that we may have life "to the full," and yet many believers are lacking this fullness and joy. Choices and circumstances have left them disillusioned, discouraged, and broken—as if casualties strewn across a blood-soaked battlefield.

Today, you may be faced with a wall as intimidating as the one Joshua and the Israelites faced. You may be entangled in some empty vice or a problem that doesn't appear to have a solution. While difficulties are an inevitable fact of life, God did not intend for His children to be defeated by them. He has placed within our hearts a longing for victory and freedom. After all, freedom is a resounding theme throughout the Bible. It is the very reason Jesus Christ came to the world, and the very purpose of His death, burial, and resurrection. The mission of God's one and only Son was to heal the brokenhearted, set free those who are in captivity, and release prisoners from darkness (Isa. 61:1). "It is for freedom that Christ has set us free," declared the apostle Paul in Galatians 5:1.

But so often, instead of turning to the One who holds the key to our freedom—the One whose Word has been tried and true since the beginning of time—we'll turn to everything else. As sheep who have wandered away from the shepherd, we meander over to a popular self-help authority. We dabble in yoga or some

New Age philosophy; we sample the latest diet fad or pour our energy into a get-rich-quick scheme. We get caught in the bramble of sin and are left feeling powerless and alone.

It's a hard road that brings a person to this point of despair and helplessness. But the truth is, at some time or another, each and every one of us will find ourselves standing before the towering walls of our own personal Jericho—in the shadow of a problem that appears insurmountable. You may be standing there today. The good news is that when you examine the lessons of this outstanding victory recorded in Joshua chapter 6, you will discover that the walls in your life are not quite as unbreakable as they seem.

THERE IS VICTORY AHEAD

The unlikely victory of the Israelites at Jericho makes it clear that no matter what you've been through up until this point—and no matter the odds stacked against you—"with God all things are possible" (Matt. 19:26). By carefully examining the Lord's instructions to His people for Jericho's defeat, we will derive seven essential keys to deepen your faith and to help you triumph over any obstacle. Without question, there is victory ahead for those who trust in the Lord and follow His perfect plan.

The Battle of Jericho lasted only seven days. Likewise, you will notice this book has seven chapters, each representing and corresponding to a specific day of battle. Please read just one chapter a day. It will be tempting to skip ahead and finish the book quickly, but your success will be directly influenced by your ability to read one chapter at a time, truly studying, soaking in, and praying over the principles you find in each one.

Every chapter opens with a short telling of a specific scene within the Jericho story, which aims to illustrate what it might have been like for the men and women involved in this historical battle. While the narratives are fictional, they are based on what we know to be true from the Bible and from archaeology. My intention is to bring the story to life for you and to set up the theme for each chapter in a unique way. You will always know when the narrative is about to start or when it has come to an end when you see a finial centered in the middle of the page.

And so the heart of our story begins. It's a pivotal moment in time for the people of God. With this legendary account in the book of Joshua comes a gift to the rest of us. Keys to conquering the impossible. Timeless secrets to overcoming any obstacle today. Journey with me as we embark on these seven important steps to success, as Joshua and the Israelites did so long ago.

DAY ONE

SHRINKING THE WALL

*Focus on the power of your Lord, not
the size of your problem.*

I imagine it may have happened something like this . . .

The Israelites wandered around the camp like zombies, a vacant gaze in their eyes as they went about their mundane tasks. If you looked closely at their faces, you would see the trails where tears had etched through the desert dust that had settled on their skin. The Israelites had wept and mourned the death of Moses for thirty days, and now their tears had run dry.

After surveying this group of disheartened men and women, Joshua disappeared into his tent and felt the weight of the entire community upon his shoulders.

"They're looking to you, Joshua," a voice said from a dim corner of the tent.

An intruder, perhaps from the nearby Hittite clan. How did this person know Joshua's name? How could he have infiltrated their company unnoticed? In an instant, Joshua was ready to fight for his life. He lunged for his sword as the figure stood and moved toward the light.

"Caleb, you startled me!" Joshua exclaimed, setting down his weapon and gripping his chest.

"I'm sorry, my friend." Caleb chuckled and placed his hand on Joshua's shoulder.

"How can you laugh at a time like this?" Joshua said.

"The days of mourning have come to an end," Caleb replied. He looked earnestly into his friend's deep-set eyes.

"Moses is dead," said Joshua, pausing as he contemplated the gravity of his statement. "You were right when you said that the people are looking to me now, but how can I dream of being all that Moses was to these men and women?"

"Joshua, you were by Moses' side as his aide from the days of your youth, learning from him. If anyone can—"

"There will never be another prophet like him among us. Ever," Joshua asserted. "The Lord sent him to do miraculous signs and wonders in Egypt. He led us out of that oppressive country. He displayed the mighty power of God in our midst. Now Moses is gone, and who am I?"

Caleb looked at Joshua with compassion. The two friends had always possessed the same indomitable spirit, the same intrepid nature. Many years earlier when Joshua and Caleb were much younger, Moses sent them out to explore Canaan, the land God had promised to His people. The ten men who had accompanied Joshua and Caleb in their reconnaissance mission were afraid and couldn't see beyond the strength and size of the Canaanites or the tough fortification of the city. Upon their return, the ten gave a negative report to the rest of the Israelites, causing fear and panic to spread throughout the entire community. The people wanted to choose a new leader and return to Egypt where they had been enslaved for so many years.

But Caleb and Joshua stood together courageously and declared to everyone in the assembly,

> The land we passed through and explored is exceedingly good. If the LORD is pleased with us, He will lead us into that land, a land flowing with milk and honey, and will give it to us. Only do not rebel against the LORD. And do not be afraid of the people of the land, because we will devour them. Their protection is gone, but the LORD is with us. Do not be afraid of them.[1]

It was a *Braveheart* moment—a scene right out of the movies. But instead of the people cheering with approval after Joshua and Caleb's speech, they threatened to stone them. That's when God stepped in. As His glory appeared suddenly at the tent of meeting, the Lord vowed that no one over the age of twenty who had grumbled against Him would enter the promised land except for Joshua and Caleb. So the Israelites wandered through the wilderness for forty years until every last rebellious person had died.

Now the two faithful comrades were on the cusp of finally realizing a dream that had been long deferred. Together they had withstood doubters, defectors, and angry mobs. But today Caleb sensed that years of heartache and hardship had shaken the confidence his friend once possessed.

"Joshua," Caleb began slowly, "before Moses died, he blessed you in the presence of all of Israel. He told you to be strong and courageous because you must go with this people into the promised land and divide it among them as their inheritance. Moses said, 'The LORD himself goes before you and will be with you; he will never leave you nor forsake you. Do not be afraid; do not be discouraged.'"[2]

These words were like medicine to Joshua's soul and seemed to awaken him from his sorrowful daze. "Thank you, Caleb," Joshua replied. "I had become so focused on Moses' absence and whether or not I was fit to take his place in leading this people through the great challenges before us."

"Yet it's not about the people or the problem," Caleb said. "It's not about Moses, and it's not about you. Everyone and everything is diminished in light of God's surpassing greatness. I just wanted to remind you of that, my friend."

And as abruptly as he had appeared in Joshua's tent, Caleb was gone, ducking under the open flap and disappearing into the crowded camp.

Soon after, Joshua received another unexpected and much-needed exhortation when the Lord spoke to him for the first time—His words filling the whole atmosphere and pushing out of sight every worry that Joshua previously had entertained. Suddenly Joshua felt incredibly small. Ashamed that he had allowed his own insecurities to take his focus off of God's greatness, Joshua fell on his face in reverence and listened intently.

The Lord said to him, "No one will be able to stand against you all the days of your life. As I was with Moses, so I will be with you; I will never leave you nor forsake you. Be strong and courageous, because you will lead these people to inherit the land I swore to their ancestors to give them."[3]

A few days later, as Joshua looked out toward the promised land, God spoke to him again, saying, "See, I have delivered Jericho into your hands, along with its king and its fighting men."[4]

He instructed Joshua to have the priests and the armed men march around the city for seven days. Then God would cause the monstrous walls to collapse before them, enabling His people to conquer Jericho as well as the other cities composing the region He swore to give their ancestors. Although Joshua didn't know how this would be possible, he knew that the Lord's greatness could accomplish any task, of any size, in any way. Ready to step out in faith and into the role of leadership Yahweh had given him, Joshua made his way over to the children of Israel to give them the plan of action.

—◆—

Wherever you are and whatever you might be going through, I'm sure your heart is about as heavy as Joshua's must have been after his beloved mentor, Moses, passed away. We know Moses was God's mediator to the people of Israel; he was esteemed as a wise leader and a doer of miracles. So when this highly revered man died, his successor, Joshua, had not only big sandals to fill but also big obstacles to overcome.

The overwhelming task set before Joshua was to lead a

company of priests and soldiers to conquer a city encompassed by impenetrable walls and inhabited by mighty men—giants, actually. In order to truly grasp the enormity of Joshua's problem, it's important for us to take a quick look at the hardships the Israelites endured leading up to this important battle.

You see, the Israelites had been enslaved and oppressed by the pharaoh and the Egyptians for more than four hundred years. That's longer than the United States of America has been a nation. But the Lord used Moses to deliver His people from Egypt, and He promised to give them a flourishing land of their own.

As they traveled to the promised land—a journey that should have taken no more than ten days—God's people quickly fell back into a life of sin and immorality (Deut. 1:2). So instead of expeditiously reaching their destination, they ended up wandering around the wilderness for forty years. Someone once suggested that the reason the Israelites wandered for so long is that the men wouldn't stop and ask for directions. All jokes aside, it's no laughing matter when God disciplines His children. Proverbs 3:12 says that, like a good father, "the Lord disciplines those he loves." Depending on our responses, that road to correction can be short, or it can be long and arduous.

For the Israelites, the journey to the promised land ended up costing a lifetime of

> THE OVERWHELMING TASK SET BEFORE JOSHUA WAS TO LEAD A COMPANY OF PRIESTS AND SOLDIERS TO CONQUER A CITY ENCOMPASSED BY IMPENETRABLE WALLS AND INHABITED BY MIGHTY MEN—GIANTS, ACTUALLY.

joy because of their doubt and disobedience. An *entire generation* missed out on the blessings the Lord had prepared for them. He had delivered His people from their oppressors, but within a short period of time they forgot about the Lord, and they began to follow idols. Instead of honoring and trusting God, they doubted, grumbled, and complained. So He allowed the Israelites to drift aimlessly across a vast desert for forty years.

BIG OBSTACLES TO OVERCOME

Once that long season of discipline was over, and after the disobedient generation had passed away, God gave His people the green light to reach Canaan. This was the promised land—a region "flowing with milk and honey" and possessing everything anyone could ever want or hope for (Ex. 3:8). After four hundred years in slavery and four decades in the desert, the Israelites were finally on its doorstep.

But there was just one last Herculean obstacle in their path: the heavily secured city of Jericho. Jericho was the gateway into the promised land. If the Israelites could somehow conquer this city, the rest would fall like carefully stacked dominos. Here's why:

> From their camp at Gilgal near the Jordan River the Israelites could see steep hills to the west. Jericho controlled the way of ascent into these mountains, and Ai, another fortress, stood at the head of the ascent. If the Israelites were to capture the hill country they must certainly take Jericho and Ai. This would put them on top of the hill country and in control of the central ridge, having driven a wedge between the northern and southern

sections of Canaan. Israel could then engage the armies of the south in battle followed by the more remote enemy in the north. But first, Jericho must fall—*and it would if Joshua and the people followed the Lord's plan of action.*[5]

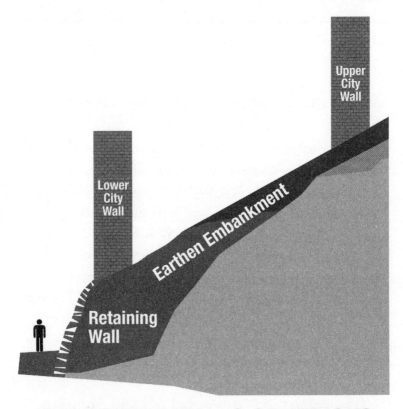

THE DOUBLE WALLS OF JERICHO
FIGURE 1

Jericho's fortitude was famed; its resources were renowned. A beautiful oasis in the midst of an otherwise barren desert, Jericho benefited from natural irrigation from the Jordan River and from the underground tributaries of the Central Mountains. Its beauty and location made Jericho ideal for trade and exchanging communication with neighboring cities. Natural defenses such as Mount Nebo to the east, the Central Mountains to the west, and the Dead Sea directly south discouraged foreign invaders.[6]

Besides all that, not one but two colossal walls surrounded Jericho. The first was a twenty-six-foot-high mud-brick wall that sat on top of a twelve- to fifteen-foot-high retaining wall at the base of an earthen embankment. The second was another twenty-six-foot-high mud-brick wall at the crest of the embankment, which placed it at about forty-six feet above ground level.[7] (See Figure 1.)

According to Joshua 6:1, these walls also featured securely barred gates to prevent anyone from coming in or out. Any way we look at it, to defeat Jericho would have been beyond the Israelites' wildest imaginations. It seemed to be an impossible obstacle.

But none of that mattered, because God is infinitely bigger than any wall or obstruction. He gave His people unusual instructions for Jericho's defeat, and He assured their victory. After announcing that He had already delivered the entire city into the hands of His people, the Lord instructed the priests and armed men to march around the city once a day for six consecutive days. Seven priests were to carry trumpets made of rams' horns as they walked in front of the ark of the covenant. Then God said:

> On the seventh day, march around the city seven times, with the priests blowing the trumpets. When you hear them sound a long blast on the trumpets, have the whole army give a loud shout; then the wall of the city will collapse and the army will go up, everyone straight in. (Josh. 6:4–5)

HOW DID JERICHO FALL?

I believe this notable city met its ultimate demise because a group of faithful men and women placed their focus and trust on the greatness of their God rather than the size of their problem. If the Israelites had relied solely on their physical sight, they would have been overwhelmed by the long list of impressive statistics that, on paper, made Jericho appear undefeatable. They could have spent every moment of their march around the city staring at how huge, how tall, how strong, how well made, and how unyielding the walls were. And if that's where their gaze had remained, they would have failed to take possession of the promised land.

Instead, the Israelites used their spiritual eyes to grasp God's greatness and to trust that He had already given them victory as He had promised. Likewise, when you and I are in the midst of a trial or storm, we have a choice about what we focus on. We tend to stare at the problem, but the longer we stare at the problem, the larger the problem becomes, causing us to feel hopeless and depressed. It's the same as a stack of past-due bills and creditors knocking at your door when you have no money. It weighs on you. And it begins to seem as though there's no way out.

Those who were afflicted with leprosy in biblical times must have felt this same kind of desperation when they looked at their awful sores and thought they would never be healed. Or Peter, who, when beckoned to walk with Jesus upon the water, took his eyes off of his Savior and began to sink beneath the tumultuous waves that surrounded him. Or the followers of Christ who saw Him nailed to the cross, the weight of sin on His shoulders. It's the all-is-lost moment in every riveting film—when it seems that the protagonist has hit rock bottom and there is no hope in sight.

What choice do we have when it appears as though help is completely out of reach? The writer of Psalm 121 told us in verses one through four:

> *I lift up my eyes to the mountains—*
> *where does my help come from?*
> *My help comes from the LORD,*
> *the Maker of heaven and earth.*
> *He will not let your foot slip—*
> *he who watches over you will not slumber;*
> *indeed, he who watches over Israel*
> *will neither slumber nor sleep.*

At any moment during your trial or struggle, you can choose to shift your focus from the mountain to the *Maker* of the mountain. Today, I encourage you to put your faith in a God who does not rest, who desires to help you, and who is bigger than any obstacle you are facing.

YOUR WALLS CAN FALL

God can and will make the walls fall down in your own personal Jericho, and the first step in accomplishing this feat hinges upon your ability to grasp His greatness. Even though it may appear that you have every disadvantage in this journey, you must set your sights on the greatness of God. Don't look at the walls that stand in your way, or you will falter and quite possibly fail. Though you may fight fear and doubt with each step you take, keep walking around those walls with your eyes fixed on

GOD CAN AND WILL MAKE THE WALLS FALL DOWN IN YOUR OWN PERSONAL JERICHO, AND THE FIRST STEP IN ACCOMPLISHING THIS FEAT HINGES UPON YOUR ABILITY TO GRASP HIS GREATNESS.

the One who has the power to flatten them with a single word from His mouth.

In reading the details of the Battle of Jericho in Joshua 6, take special note of the first verse, which reads, "Now the gates of Jericho were securely barred because of the Israelites. No one went out and no one came in." A notoriously strong city was entirely shut up. It was quiet. The gates were securely barred. Not a single person was allowed to come in or out. Why was that? We discover the reason in Joshua 2:1–11 when two Israelite spies went into Jericho to survey the kingdom. A prostitute named Rahab hid the Israelite spies on her rooftop, and this is what she said to them:

> A great fear of you has fallen on us, so that all who live in this country are melting in fear because of you. We have heard how the LORD dried up the water of the Red Sea for you when you came out of Egypt, and what you did to Sihon and Og, the two kings of the Amorites east of the Jordan, whom you completely destroyed. When we heard of it, our hearts melted in fear and everyone's courage failed because of you, for the LORD your God is God in heaven above and on the earth below. (vv. 9–11)

When you were just a child, did you ever squirm at the sight of a spider or an insect that had gotten a little too close for comfort? If so, perhaps your mom or dad attempted to bolster your courage by saying, "You know, that bug is more afraid of you than you are of it." Well, it was similar with the people of Jericho versus the people of Israel. If God's people harbored any fear as they marched around the outside of that city and looked up at the gigantic walls, the people inside that city, looking down at God's people, had greater fear. Their gates were tightly shut because they were afraid of the Israelites. Better stated, they were afraid of the Israelites' God. The reputation of God—the miracles He had done and the ability He had given His people to conquer their enemies—preceded the Israelites' arrival in Jericho. It reached the ears of the Jerichoites, striking fear into their hearts. They knew that God was *great*.

————

There's a wonderful story behind an old mariner's chart located at the British Museum in London. The chart shows the coast of North America in the year 1525 with intriguing notations written by a cartographer on unexplored areas of the map. He wrote, "Here be giants," "Here be fiery scorpions," and "Here be dragons." The map eventually came to be owned by Sir John Franklin, a British Royal Navy officer and Arctic explorer, in the early 1800s. Perhaps he knew the Lord, because he scratched out the fearful inscriptions and wrote across them: "Here is GOD!"[8]

Whenever you are traveling through daunting or uncharted territory, gaze upon the greatness of God. Your problem will shrink faster than a sugar cube in a rainstorm as you walk daily understanding His infinite magnitude and aptitude. It's about proper perspective.

A young shepherd boy named David had the right perspective, and it led to his unlikely victory in a very unbalanced matchup recorded in 1 Samuel 17. David was a teenager—not a soldier—and yet he chose to confront Goliath, a mighty Philistine warrior who stood more than nine feet tall. David was the underdog by every measure, while Goliath was the undisputed heavyweight champion of the world.

The Bible says that whenever Goliath hurled insults at the Israelite soldiers at the battle lines, daring one of them to stand up to him, they all ran away from him in great fear. But David said to Saul, the king of Israel whom David later would succeed, "Let no one lose heart on account of this Philistine; your servant will go and fight him" (1 Sam. 17:32). Despite King Saul's doubts, David assured him that since God had enabled him to defeat a lion and a bear that had attacked his father's sheep as he tended them, God also would help him defeat Goliath.

David's memory of past victories provided the confidence for his future victories. So when it came time to fight the Philistine champion who had struck terror into the hearts of his kinsmen, David shouted boldly to Goliath:

> You come against me with sword and spear and javelin, but I come against you in the name of the LORD Almighty, the God of the armies of Israel, whom you have defied. This day the LORD will deliver you into my hands, and I'll strike you down and cut off your head. (1 Sam. 17:45–46)

Then as Goliath moved closer to David to attack him, the Bible says David ran toward the giant. He struck Goliath down and killed him instantly with a single stone from his slingshot.

David was one bad brother. Can you say *amen* to that? He analyzed the problem and knew that in comparison to the enormous God he served, Goliath was nothing more than a gnat. In fact,

David was so confident in the Lord's deliverance that he declared boldly, "All those gathered here will know that it is not by sword or spear that the LORD saves; for the battle is the LORD's, and he will give all of you into our hands" (1 Sam. 17:47).

It's the same for you. You must be consumed by the greatness of God and trust that the battle is His in order to defeat the giant standing in your way. So who is this God who we cling to?

1. GOD IS THE CREATOR OF THE UNIVERSE.

Attempting to understand who God is would be impossible without discussing the wonder of His creation. To behold the rushing waters of the Niagara Falls and the snowcapped Rocky Mountains would give you a small glimpse. To experience the underwater dreamland of the Great Barrier Reef and the teeming wildlife of the Amazon rainforest would give you a clue.

How accurately King David spoke of the infinite number of stars in the universe when he said in Psalm 19:1, "The heavens declare the glory of God; the skies proclaim the work of his hands."[9] And we haven't even mentioned the pièce de résistance of creation: man. Our bodies boast trillions of cells,[10] and the human mind is more complex than any computer system ever made. Volumes have been written about the intricacy of our circulatory, endocrine, immune, lymphatic, digestive, skeletal, muscular, respiratory, and nervous systems—not to mention the sheer miracle of our reproductive process.

One day during a trip to Beijing, I sat on top of the Great Wall of China and tried to explain the concept of a Creator God to a girl whom I will call Mei. Imagine never being told that God existed or that He created you, the earth, and everything in it, as well as the galaxies. As I write, Mei is among more than 1.3 billion people who live in China, most of whom have never had the chance to hear the truth about Jesus Christ due to the country's restrictions on religious freedoms. So, with the help of an interpreter, I began to speak with Mei about God. It dawned on me as we were sitting on the Great Wall of China that I could convey the idea of God as Creator with a simple illustration. I took off my sunglasses and held them in my hand.

"Where did these sunglasses come from? Did they grow on a tree and someone gathered them and decided to sell them at the shop, or did someone make them?" I asked her.

"Someone made them," she replied.

"Right. You and I have never seen anyone make these sunglasses, and yet we believe that someone made them."

Mei nodded in agreement, so I continued. Taking off my watch, I asked her the same question, and she concurred that someone had made the watch, that it didn't just sprout from the ground all by its lonesome. Then I held the sunglasses in one hand and the watch in the other hand.

"Which is more complex to create, my watch or my sunglasses?" I asked.

Without hesitation, Mei pointed to the watch.

Next, I pulled my laptop out of its carrying case. "Have you ever seen a computer growing on a tree like an orange or on a vine like a tomato?"

"No," she said. "Someone made the computer."

"So which is more complex?" I asked her. "This computer or the watch?"

Mei pointed to the computer. Then I said, "Now which is more complex and advanced, the computer or *you*?" It didn't take Mei but a half a second to point to herself.

"In the same way that someone had to make the sunglasses and the watch and the computer," I shared, "someone had to make you."

Then, I looked around the Chinese countryside, at the lush mountains beneath the hazy sky above us. The Great Wall meandered through this gorgeous backdrop for miles and miles—as far as the eye could see. It is the world's largest military structure and underwent construction off and on from 220 bc to 1644.[11] Perched atop a precarious ridge, it's a wonder how ancient builders managed to climb to this location, let alone transport heavy stones and equipment there. After climbing a series of steep steps, travelers today must take a cable car to get to the top of this mammoth structure. That's probably why the Great Wall is China's most popular tourist destination and one of the Seven Wonders of the World.

Though it seemed I had run out of props for my little game of comparisons, I turned to Mei and asked her one final question. "Which is more complex?" I started. "Which is greater and more important, the wall on top of the mountain or the mountain underneath the wall?"

She paused as she pondered the question, and then she said, "The mountain." It seemed as though something had clicked in her mind. We have all these man-made objects—from something as simple as a pair of sunglasses to something as advanced as a laptop computer or one of man's most remarkable feats of engineering, the Great Wall of China. And yet, the mountain beneath all those items I described was greater still. Someone had to have made that mountain. Moreover, someone had to have made you and me. And I think that was the first time in Mei's life anyone had explained to her that there was a Creator God. If our heavenly Father cared enough about us to create us in the first place, He certainly cares enough about our problems to help us in our times of need. I see God's greatness in creation.

2. GOD IS EVERYWHERE AT ALL TIMES.

Some time ago, a woman wrote to *Reader's Digest* about her son Doug, who was looking out his bedroom window at a full moon just before bedtime. The young boy asked his mother if God was in the moon.

"God is everywhere," she said.

"Is God in my tummy?" Doug asked.

Not knowing where these questions were leading, his mother replied, "Sort of . . ."

Then Doug announced, "Well, God wants a banana!"[12]

We can feel very childlike when attempting to comprehend the omnipresence of God. One of the simplest ways to explain the Lord's omnipresent nature is to say that He is everywhere at all times. In our humanness, we think in terms of the location and material composition of a person or an object. So it's difficult for us to fathom that God exists outside of space and time and that He is present everywhere at the same time. Yet our heavenly Father is not material as we are. In fact, Jesus revealed, "God is spirit, and his worshipers must worship in the Spirit and in truth" (John 4:24).

There's no place in the entire universe we can escape God or hide from His presence. Psalm 139 is one of the best examples of this profound truth, particularly verses seven through ten:

> *Where can I go from your Spirit?*
> *Where can I flee from your presence?*
> *If I go up to the heavens, you are there;*
> *if I make my bed in the depths, you are there.*

If I rise on the wings of the dawn,
  if I settle on the far side of the sea,
even there your hand will guide me,
  your right hand will hold me fast.

There is no corner of the world where God's presence cannot reach—no niche in the universe that can elude Him. But because we can't see God in physical form, there may be times when we feel like King David when he wrote in Psalm 13:1, "How long, LORD? Will you forget me forever? How long will you hide your face from me?" When we are in the depths of sorrow or despair, it can feel as though God is absent, but His silence should never be mistaken for absence. He is always there, always concerned, always desiring a deep and abiding relationship with us. He is genuinely and authentically interested in our troubles and trials. "Cast all your anxiety on him because he cares for you" (1 Peter 5:7).

God's triune nature as Father, Son, and Holy Spirit is the ultimate realization of His omnipresence. To attempt to fathom the Trinity is about as mind-boggling as trying to understand the Lord's omnipresence. I don't expect to fully explain either doctrine within this small section of this book, but I hope I can at least shed a little light on the topic.

God was present here on earth in an intimate way when He sent His Son Jesus to live among us in the flesh, coming down to our level in a tangible form. Men, women, and children were able to *see* Him and find compassion and forgiveness, *touch* Him and be

THERE IS NO CORNER OF THE WORLD WHERE GOD'S PRESENCE CANNOT REACH—NO NICHE IN THE UNIVERSE THAT CAN ELUDE HIM.

healed, and *hear* His voice and receive the truth. He is Immanuel, "God with us" (Matt. 1:23).

And while all this was happening, God was still God in heaven, seated upon His throne in power and sovereignty. We know this to be true because, while Jesus said He and the Father are one (John 17:11), He prayed to the Father many times during His time on earth. Read Matthew 26:36–46, Mark 1:35, and Luke 3:21, 5:16, 6:12, and 9:28 for a few examples.

After Jesus rose from the dead and before He went up to heaven, He promised He would send the Holy Spirit in His place to fill our hearts, empower us, and guide us. Christ called the Spirit "the Helper" in John 14:26 (NKJV). If you are a believer, the Spirit of God resides with you everywhere you go, helping you through whatever obstacles you may be facing today.

3. GOD KNOWS EVERY DETAIL.

My dad is my hero. He is the greatest preacher I have ever known. He has been a faithful husband, father, brother, son, and minister for more than five decades. When I was growing up, my dad had the uncanny ability of knowing *everything*. Maybe your mother or father was the same way. You've heard a parent or teacher say he or she had eyes in the back of his or her head, right? Well, I'm certain my dad had two sets of eyes in the back of his head because he always knew exactly what was going on among my four siblings and me.

One day, my youngest brother, Deano, and I were playing basketball outside in the front driveway with a couple of friends. We used to play every day before and after school, and we usually spent more time arguing about the other person's biased calls than actually shooting baskets.

On this particular day, I decided that I was going to wear my dad's brand-new Chuck Taylor All Star sneakers while Deano and I played basketball. These shoes were sweet—a vanilla-colored canvas with bright-white rubber toes, sidewalls, and laces. I was wearing them without my dad's permission, of course, but he was never going to find out. You see, I put on three or four pairs of socks so that if my feet became sweaty, the moisture wouldn't leave a stain. Then I swept off the driveway perfectly. I eliminated every grain of sand, pebble, and twig because I didn't want the shoes to get scuffed. Let me tell you, I had never looked so cool walking onto that pristine driveway with those new Chuck Taylors laced up.

So my brother and I were in the middle of our basketball game, and we started fighting as usual. I don't remember what I said or did, but he got really angry and stormed into the open garage. I continued playing with my other buddies, and the next thing I knew, someone yelled, "Look out!" Deano threw something at me. As it hurled through the air, I could see from the corner of my eye that the thrown object was large and shiny. It looked heavy, like a piece of equipment of some kind. The mysterious item landed two or three feet in front of me. He missed. Phew! Crisis averted . . . or so I thought. It was a can of paint, and when it hit the ground, the lid popped off—spraying black paint everywhere.

I looked down at my feet, and one of my dad's shoes was covered in solid black paint. I knew at that moment I was a dead man. When my dad came home later that evening, you better believe I received a well-deserved punishment. Dad would always find out what we were up to, whether it was easy to cover up or not so easy to hide, like black paint all over his brand-new white sneaker.

As much as I believed my dad knew everything when I was a child, I know now as an adult that our human knowledge, understanding, and wisdom are completely inadequate when compared to God's omniscience. The Lord alone knows all things. He knows the measurements of the universe, the lifespan of each star, the rotation of the planets. He knows the temperature in New Mexico, the temperature in the earth's core, and the temperature on the moon. He knows the price of tea in China. He knows the number of hairs on your head—even if that number is zero. "Nothing in all creation is hidden from God's sight," attests Hebrews 4:13. "Everything is uncovered and laid bare before the eyes of him to whom we must give account."

God knows concepts and information that our limited human minds could never grasp, things that are impossible for me to write about. And beyond all that knowledge, He is wise. There's a difference between knowledge and wisdom. Beyond having an acquaintance with facts and principles (knowledge), God is the supreme authority in discerning what is true and right (wisdom). He knows what will bring fruitfulness and what will bring destruction. He knows what will bring success and what will bring failure. And He has shared much of this wisdom with us in His Word, the Bible. God's wisdom is freely available to us within those sacred pages, which is why we need to have our noses in the Word every single day—especially when we are experiencing difficult times.

EVEN THOUGH WE MAY NOT UNDERSTAND THE GREATNESS OF GOD, HE CHOOSES TO LAVISH GREATNESS UPON US, NOT JUST SO THAT HE CAN RECEIVE GLORY AND REVERENCE, BUT ALSO BECAUSE HE *LOVES* US.

In His omniscience, God knows the ins and outs of the wall you're up against and how to bring it down. This truth leads you to trust not only in His knowledge and wisdom but also in the strategy He has already prescribed for your victory. How awesome that we serve an omniscient God who is willing to share His knowledge with us so that we can conquer the impossible obstacles in our lives.

4. GOD IS ALL-POWERFUL.

God is capable of anything. He can crush solar systems with a thought or eradicate the cosmos with a word. (Since He spoke the universe into existence [Gen. 1 and John 1:1–14], He most certainly could do the opposite.) He can harness lightning and thunder and unleash torrential rains. If He so desired, the Lord God Almighty could cause the oceans to boil or the atmosphere to freeze. No creature in this universe is more powerful than God, for He is the one who created everything.

God demonstrated His omnipotence time and time again throughout the pages of the Bible. The first sentence in Genesis magnifies the Lord's wondrous power when He created the entire universe—heavens, earth, oceans, lakes, rivers, plants, trees, innumerable species of mammals, sea creatures, birds, insects, and man. He accomplished this in a mere six days. This same God caused a forty-day storm that flooded the earth and spared His righteous servant, Noah; his family; and two of every species of living creature (Gen. 7). He spoke to Moses through a bush that burned yet was not consumed (Ex. 3). He sent ten terrible plagues to the land of Egypt because Pharaoh would not set His people free (Ex. 7–12).

The Lord sweetened the bitter waters of Marah so His people could drink it (Ex. 15), divided the Red Sea so the Israelites could pass through it and escape the Egyptians (Ex. 14), and made flakes of bread fall from the sky every morning to feed them (Ex. 16). Skipping over to Joshua chapter 3, we discover the reason *why* God chose to reveal His power here on earth.

On the journey to Jericho, the Israelites came upon a huge obstacle—the Jordan River, which is approximately 223 miles long.[13] (This is the same river in which Jesus Christ was baptized later in Matthew 3:13–17.) Crossing over the Jordan surely would have been dangerous and nearly impossible, especially since the river was at flood stage (Josh. 3:15; 4:18). So what did God do? He caused the water that was flowing downstream to be cut off and stand up in a heap so that the Israelites could cross over on dry land, just as He did when they needed to cross the Red Sea (Josh. 3:15–17).

God does not often explain Himself, nor does He need to, but in Joshua 4:24 He chose to reveal two reasons for this miracle: "He did this so that all the peoples of the earth might know that the hand of the LORD is powerful and so that you might always fear the LORD your God."

First, God wanted to demonstrate His omnipotence in the sight of the world. Second, He desired to be greatly revered by His people. What sort of obstacle is a river at flood stage when God's awesome power is always overflowing? That river is reduced to a faucet that is turned off with the flick of one's wrist. A raging sea is calmed in an instant when Jesus Christ, the manifestation of our heavenly Father's omnipotence here on earth, uttered three simple words: "Quiet! Be still!" (Mark 4:39). This power—embodied by God's one and only Son—gave sight to the blind, speech to the mute, hearing to the deaf, healing to the sick, mobility to the disabled, and forgiveness to the sinner. It conquered sin, and ultimately death, as Jesus Christ was crucified for our transgressions and was raised to new life on the third day.

It is important for you to know that God is omnipotent because at some point in your life, you may feel as if your problem is irreversible and your situation unsalvageable. It may feel as if no one in the world is able to save you. But there is no situation that God cannot repair; there is no hurdle He cannot surmount and no person He cannot save. If we could only put our trust in the limitless power of God, then we would never have a reason to worry or fear in the face of walls that crumble in His presence.

John Piper said:

> If you don't see the greatness of God then all the things that money can buy become very exciting. If you can't see the sun, you will be impressed with a streetlight. If you've never felt thunder and lightning, you'll be impressed with fireworks. And if you turn your back on the greatness and majesty of God, you'll fall in love with a world of shadows and short-lived pleasures.[14]

Nothing compares to God. Nothing satisfies except for Him. And nothing besides Him will give us complete victory. That is why it's so critical that the first step toward conquering our impossible obstacles must be taken while in total captivation of our majestic Lord's greatness.

OBSTACLES ARE OPPORTUNITIES

Think about something for a moment: If there weren't a wall standing in your way today, how would you be able to give glory to God for the victory He wants to give you in the future? How would you be able to praise God in the sight of your friends and neighbors for providing for you, healing you, forgiving you, giving you grace, or coming through for you in the nick of time?

No one is exempt from the inevitable problems of the world. Not even followers of Jesus. Christ Himself said unequivocally in John 16:33, "I have told you these things, so that in me you may have peace. In this world you will have trouble. But take heart! I have overcome the world."

Unless we have trials and obstacles to defeat, what other opportunity would we have to cultivate our character and to increase our faith? And what other opportunity would the Lord have to demonstrate His surpassing creativity, omnipresence, omniscience, and omnipotence personally in our lives?

Whatever difficulty you may be facing, let 2 Chronicles 16:9 encourage and embolden you: "For the eyes of the LORD range throughout the earth *to strengthen* those whose hearts are fully committed to him" (emphasis added). Enduring hardship gives us an occasion to show ourselves loyal to God, and it gives God an occasion to show Himself strong on our behalf.

The number-one prayer request I hear from expectant parents is for their baby to be healthy and strong. Strength is a virtue. It is of great worth. We all want to be strong and for our children to be strong, but how many of us realize that trials are a necessary precursor to gaining strength?

Thirty-three times in the Bible we find the charge, "Be strong."[15] In Joshua 1:2–9, God told the new leader to be strong and courageous three times, which echoed Moses' final words to Joshua in Deuteronomy 31:6. Sometimes we can be so thickheaded that we need to hear an important piece of information more than once. God also gave Joshua the assurance that no one would be able to stand against him all the days of his life, and that He would never leave him or forsake him (Josh. 1:15).

Perhaps you are saying, "Well, Dudley, God gave that promise to Joshua; He didn't give it to me." Not so. You and I can take this assurance to heart because it's repeated twice in the New Testament—once as Jesus' departing words in Matthew 28:20 and again in Hebrews 13:5. God will never abandon you in the midst of your troubles, and He wants you to rely upon His greatness.

James Hudson Taylor, a nineteenth-century British Christian missionary to China, put it this way: "How many estimate difficulties in the light of their own resources, and thus attempt little and often fail in the little they attempt! All God's giants have been weak men, who did great things for God because they reckoned on His being with them."[16]

What if, instead of allowing ourselves to become discouraged by every obstacle we encountered, we simply view each one as an opportunity for us and for others to see God's greatness in action? "Whom else do you know," wrote Sam Storms, "that is high, yet humble; strong, yet sensitive; righteous, yet gracious; powerful, yet merciful; authoritative, yet tender; holy, yet forgiving; just, yet compassionate; angry, yet gentle; [and] firm, yet friendly?"[17] So in the face of adversity, let us throw our every hope into the arms of this capable and magnificent God.

THERE ARE NOT ENOUGH WORDS

Even though I've sought to encapsulate the facets of God's greatness into the confines of this chapter, the truth is that we never will be able to fully perceive the totality of His incomparable nature.

Dr. S. M. Lockridge was the pastor of Calvary Baptist Church in San Diego, California, from 1953 to 1993. He graduated to heaven in the year 2000, but he is well-known for a passage out of his sermon titled "That's My King," in which he ventured to describe all the marvelous qualities our Lord possesses. I encourage you to look up Lockridge's famous sermon on the Internet and listen to it in his own voice. It's quite beautiful. Here is an excerpt:

My King is the key of knowledge. He's the well-spring of wisdom. He's the doorway of deliverance. He's the pathway of peace. He's the roadway of righteousness. He's the highway of holiness. He's the gateway of glory. He's the master of the mighty. He's the captain of the conquerors. He's the head of the heroes. He's the leader of the legislators. He's the overseer of the overcomers. He's the governor of governors. He's the prince of princes. He's the King of Kings and He's the Lord of Lords . . .

His life is matchless. His goodness is limitless. His mercy is everlasting. His love never changes. His word is enough. His grace is sufficient. His reign is righteous. His yoke is easy and His burden is light. I wish I could describe Him to you. He's indescribable. He's indescribable. He's incomprehensible. He's invincible. He's irresistible. I'm trying to tell you, the heaven of heavens cannot contain Him, let alone a man explain Him. You can't get Him out of your mind. You can't get Him off of your hands. You can't outlive Him, and you can't live without Him. The Pharisees couldn't stand Him, but they found out they couldn't stop Him. Pilate couldn't find any fault in Him . . . Herod couldn't kill Him. Death couldn't handle Him, and the grave couldn't hold Him. That's my King!

He always has been, and He always will be. I'm talking

about He had no predecessor and He'll have no successor.
There was nobody before Him and there'll be nobody after
Him. You can't impeach Him, and He's not going to resign.
That's my King! . . . Thine is the Kingdom and the power and
the glory for ever, and ever. And when you get through with all
of the forevers, then Amen.[18]

As superb as his composition is, Lockridge's point was that there
aren't enough words in any language that can adequately capture
God's greatness. Saint Augustine, who lived from AD 354 to 430,
came across the same conundrum as he endeavored to write about the
Lord's triune nature of the Father, Son, and Holy Spirit.[19] Dr. Stephen
Seamands, a professor of Christian doctrine at Asbury Theological
Seminary, described the marvelous epiphany Augustine had:

Earlier I mentioned Augustine's monumental *On the Trinity*,
which he worked on for fifteen years. Shortly after he completed
it, he was walking along the Mediterranean shore on the coast
of North Africa when he chanced upon a boy who kept filling a
bucket with seawater and pouring it into a large hole in the sand.

"Why are you doing that?" Augustine asked the boy.

"I'm pouring the Mediterranean Sea into the hole," the boy
replied in all seriousness.

"My dear boy, what an impossible thing to try to do!"
chided Augustine. "The sea is far too vast, and your hole is far
too small."

Then as Augustine continued his walk, it dawned on him
that in his efforts to write on the Trinity, he was much like that
boy: the subject was far too vast, and his mind far too small!

The Trinity establishes and proclaims the mystery of God;

it reminds us that we cannot fully fathom the unfathomable. In life and ministry it is important to learn what we *cannot* know. The Trinity teaches us to acknowledge and embrace the limits of our knowledge.[20]

But here is what we do know: even though we may not understand the greatness of God, He chooses to lavish greatness upon us not just so that He can receive glory and reverence, but also because He *loves* us. The Lord God Almighty, the Creator of the universe, loves you. He loves you so much that He gave His one and only Son Jesus as a sacrifice for your sins and mine, so that we could be forgiven (Matt. 26:28), have abundant life (John 10:10 NKJV), and spend eternity in heaven with Him (John 3:16). Isn't that what is truly unfathomable—that a God in heaven loves you so much that He spared no expense for you?

"From everlasting to everlasting the LORD's love is with those who fear him," declares Psalm 103:17, "and his righteousness with their children's children." This is the crux of the whole matter. To fully comprehend the Lord's greatness is absolutely useless unless you believe that He has elected to reserve the greatest facet of His nature—His love—just for you. Need further proof? Take a look at Jeremiah 31:3: "The LORD appeared to us in the past, saying: 'I have loved you with an everlasting love; I have drawn you with unfailing kindness.'" And 1 John 4:8 puts it simply: "God is love."

Yes, the Lord wants to demonstrate His greatness in your life. He wants to help you to conquer the impossible obstacles that stand in the way of your victory. But the overarching reason *why* God moves on your behalf in these ways is because of His great love for you.

You may not understand everything fully, but trust in the Lord.

He is in all places, knows all things, and is able to accomplish any task. What reason, then, do you have to fear any wall that may be standing in your way? Before today, that problem seemed hopeless. Now that you've caught a glimpse of God's greatness, you know He "is able to do immeasurably more than all we ask or imagine, according to his power that is at work within us" (Eph. 3:20). The inherent greatness of Almighty God will cause the walls in your life to shrink in an instant, and this proper perspective is the first step to ultimate victory.

⌐

As Joshua and the Israelites looked up at the airtight walls of Jericho, they may not have been completely able to comprehend God's greatness, but they trusted that God was great. After they marched around their enemy's city that first day, not one pebble had moved from the structure, but still they trusted. For a generation of people who spent their entire lives wandering in the wilderness, these stone walls presented a challenge that they never could have imagined. Yet, against the backdrop of the wonders they had seen God accomplish, those walls didn't stand so tall. They might as well have been made of Legos.

A PRAYER FOR TODAY

Father in Heaven, I want to take this time to praise You because You are awesome and wonderful. You are the Creator of the entire universe. You are in all places at all times; You are all-knowing and all-powerful. Any obstacle I face now or will face in the future instantly shrinks in light of Your greatness. Thank You for loving me so much that You desire to be my God and have a relationship with me. I'm so thankful for the miracles You have done for me in the past and the miracles You are about to do. Help me always to put my trust solely in Your goodness and Your greatness. In Jesus' name I pray, amen.

DAY TWO

AN UNCONVENTIONAL PLAN

Trust in God's plan even when it doesn't make sense.

F or Rahab, the simple task of grocery shopping had become rather complicated over the years. She couldn't buy dried fruit from the merchant in the center of the market because of his wife's suspicions, so she had to trek to the far end of the market to purchase apricots and dates from another retailer. Her exchange with the spice seller was always discreet since they had worked out a special arrangement. And she never knew when she might bump into a man in the light of day with whom she had become quite familiar under the cover of night. Young men, older men, middle-class merchants, and upper-class noblemen— there was no discrimination of age or economic status as far as Rahab's list of clientele was concerned.

"Rahab the prostitute." Her reputation preceded her. Throughout the course of her life, many of her fellow Jerichoites had reminded her that she would never be anything other than a paramour. But that was all about to change.

Arriving at home to prepare her newly purchased ingredients for supper that evening, Rahab heard a sudden knock at her front door. *Who could it be at this hour?* she thought. None of her customers knew where she lived, for she always met them in secret locations.

"I'll get it!" she called to her mother, who was in the other room.

When Rahab opened the door and saw the two strangers standing before her, she somehow knew instantly who they were. In town earlier that day, rumors swirled about two men, Israelites, who had come to spy on their land. Usually the rumors were about her, so it was refreshing to have the gossip shift for once in her adult life!

At the market, the Jerichoites nervously spoke of how the God of the Israelites had dried a path in the middle of the Red Sea for them when they fled from Egypt. This mighty God had destroyed the Amorite kings, Sihon and Og, and was more powerful than any other god in heaven or on earth. In fact, it was possible that there was no other God besides Him! He caused the people of Israel to succeed in all they had set out to do, and it was rumored that He had given Jericho into their hands.

And now, the two Israelite spies were standing before Rahab. Having been in the company of powerful men, she knew how to appear calm and at ease. "Please come in," she said.

The two strangers made their way inside the house as Rahab looked outside to see if anyone had been watching. She closed the door and clasped her hands together so they would stop shaking.

"Don't be afraid," said the stouter of the two. "We need a place to stay for the night."

"Yes, of course," Rahab replied.

"Who are these men, Rahab?" her mother asked in their native language, coming into the room with Rahab's younger brothers.

"Mama, everything is alright."

A cough resonated from the back room.

"That's Baba," Rahab said to the men. "My father. He is bedridden."

Meanwhile, Yassib, Rahab's youngest brother, had quietly made his way over to the stout spy and reached out to touch his cloak when Rahab saw him in her periphery. "Yassib, don't even think about it!" she scolded.

Yassib giggled and ran away to hide behind Mama. His teenage brother, Tarek, gave him a playful thump on the head for daring to get a closer look at the foreigners.

"Mama, when I was at the market today, everyone was talking about these men," Rahab explained. "They are the spies from Israel."

"Spies from Israel?" Yassib shouted.

"Shh!" Rahab and her mother said simultaneously. Tarek gave Yassib another thump on the head.

"They are the reason the whole city is afraid," Rahab continued. "Their God has done many miraculous signs and wonders for them."

"We will not harm you or your family," said the slender spy who sported a thick beard. "We simply need a place to stay overnight."

Rahab's mother turned and whispered to her, "Do whatever

they want, and maybe we will be spared from the calamity that is coming upon this city."

Her daughter nodded. "We are happy to have you," she told the men. "You're safe here in our home."

Just then, there was a forceful knock at the door.

"Are you expecting someone?" one of the men asked Rahab, placing his hand on the grip of his sword.

"Quickly, Tarek, take these men to the roof and hide them under the stalks of flax," Rahab told her brother. "Yassib, go into the other room with Baba and do not come out under any circumstance."

The boys did as they were told, and Mama went over to the kitchen area to busy herself. Rahab quickly applied eyeliner in the mirror and swept her long hair over one shoulder before going to the door. Another forceful knock. She took a deep breath and opened the door to reveal a messenger and two tall soldiers from the king's palace.

"Are you Rahab the prostitute?" a soldier asked.

Rahab ignored the sinking feeling in her stomach that always came when people called her that. "Yes," she said.

The men pushed past her and into the house, looking around with intense scrutiny.

"If you tell me what you are looking for, perhaps I can assist you," Rahab said as she touched the royal messenger's forearm gently. She hoped to use her professional skills in seduction to distract the soldiers from seeing something that might put her guests in danger. The messenger stepped away from her and did not look at her when he spoke.

"The king sends word to bring out the men who came to

you and entered your house because they have come to spy out the entire land," he said.

"The men came to me, but I did not know where they had come from," Rahab replied. "They left when it was time to close the city gate. That was not too long ago."

Suddenly, a not-so-subtle creak came from the roof. One of the soldiers looked up at the ceiling, incredulity etched into his chiseled face. He made his way to the window. The home in which Rahab and her family lived was built against the city wall and had an advantageous view of the gate.

"Listen," said Rahab, "I don't know which way the spies went, but go after them quickly. You may catch up with them."

The royal messenger studied Rahab's face for a moment and looked over at the soldier who had been peering out the window. The soldier gave him the "all clear" sign, and without a word, the men set out in pursuit of the spies on the road that led to the fords of the Jordan. Rahab closed the door behind them. She leaned against it and took a deep breath.

"You did well, my daughter," Mama said.

Yassib ran back into the room cheering for his sister, and Tarek returned from the rooftop. Together they finished preparing dinner and Rahab took a plate up to the Israelites.

"Thank you for your hospitality and courage," the men said to her.

Rahab crouched low and spoke softly. "I know that the LORD has given you this land," she began, "and that all who live in Jericho are melting in fear because of you. I know that the LORD your God is God in heaven above and on the earth below. Now then, please swear to me by the LORD that you will show kindness to my family, because I have shown kindness to you. Give me a sure sign that you will spare the lives of my father and mother, my brothers and sisters, and all who belong to them— and that you will save us from death."[1]

"Our lives for your lives!" the men assured her. "If you don't tell what we are doing, we will treat you kindly and faithfully when the LORD gives us the land."[2]

Just before dawn, the spies came back down to the house from the rooftop. One of the men removed his necklace made of braided leather and placed it around Yassib's neck.

"Be good to your mother and your sister," he said to the boy.

Yassib nodded and ran to Baba's room to show off his new badge of honor. Then, the other spy handed Rahab a scarlet cord and instructed her to tie it in her window once the Lord's people had entered Jericho, in order to bind the oath they had made. He told her to bring her entire family into her house and not to allow any of them to go outside during the siege.

"And if you tell anyone what we are doing," he reminded her, "we will be released from the oath you made us swear."

"Let it be as you say," Rahab agreed. "Now, go to the hills so the pursuers will not find you. Hide yourselves there three days until they return, and then go on your way."[3]

She carefully lowered the spies by a rope through the window. As she watched them depart stealthily before the sun illuminated the valley, she tied the scarlet cord in the window and marveled at the thought of God's salvation and mercy toward her and her family.

The story of Rahab and the Israelite spies teaches us that the Lord can involve anyone in His unique plan who chooses to put his or her faith and trust in Him. God's grace, demonstrated through His special purpose, can even extend to someone of a disreputable position such as a prostitute. Rahab was discounted and disdained. Stuck in a lifestyle that offered no hope of ever changing. Judged by her countrymen and women at every turn. But then, the grace of God came to her in the form of two strangers who knocked on her door one night. They didn't want her body; they simply wanted a place to stay—to be under cover of a different kind. Because of Rahab's trust in the God of the Israelites, she became part of His unique plan to give victory to His people—and she and her entire household were then spared from the calamity that came upon Jericho.

If God had a plan to change the life of a Jericho prostitute, then He most certainly has a plan for you. Do you believe that? You say, "Dudley, you don't know what I've been through, and you don't know the things I've done." The next time you think the Lord can't use you within His sovereign plan, consider this: Jacob conned his own brother out of his birthright. Joseph was a boastful dreamer. John the Baptist ate bugs and wore weird clothing. Moses was a mess—he murdered an Egyptian man, and when God chose him to lead the Israelites out of Egypt, he stuttered and made excuses. David stole another man's wife and sent the man to the frontlines of battle to be killed. Peter was fickle, impulsive, and denied Christ three times. Martha worried too much. Paul was overly zealous about the law and rigorously persecuted Christians.

Yet God, in His great mercy and unfailing love, is a master at taking the pieces of our brokenness and failures and transforming

> YET GOD, IN HIS GREAT MERCY AND UNFAILING LOVE, IS A MASTER AT TAKING THE PIECES OF OUR BROKENNESS AND FAILURES AND TRANSFORMING THEM INTO A BEAUTIFUL MOSAIC FOR HIS GLORY.

them into a beautiful mosaic for His glory. He says in 2 Corinthians 12:9, "My grace is sufficient for you, for my power is made perfect in weakness," which indicates that it's not about our pasts or our failures, but about what He can do despite all those things. I don't think our heavenly Father has any interest in beating you over the head with the labels others have given you or the shortcomings of which you are well aware. I think what He is primarily concerned with is getting you to embrace the fact that He has a plan for your life. It may be unconventional, but it's still a plan. And when you follow God's plan, that's when you will find true joy, peace, and victory.

IT STARTS WITH A PROMISE

God's plan begins with a promise. It goes back further than the promise the two spies made to preserve the lives of Rahab and her family once the Israelites conquered Jericho. It goes back to a monumental promise that almighty God Himself made to a righteous man named Abraham, the patriarch of Israel who had the honor of being called "God's friend" (James 2:23). This is the seven-part promise that the Lord made to Abraham in Genesis 12:1–3:

> Go from your country, your people and your father's household to the land I will show you.

I will make you into a great nation,
    and I will bless you;
I will make your name great,
    and you will be a blessing.
I will bless those who bless you,
    and whoever curses you I will curse;
    and all peoples on earth
will be blessed through you.

God reaffirmed this promise to Abraham's son Isaac, then to Isaac's son Jacob, then to Moses who led the Israelites out of Egypt. He told Moses in Deuteronomy 7:1 that He would bring the people into a land they would possess and drive out "seven nations larger and stronger than you." And pay special attention to what the Lord said in Deuteronomy 9:1:

> You are now about to cross the Jordan to go in and dispossess nations greater and stronger than you, with large cities that have walls up to the sky.

Sounds like Jericho, doesn't it? Jericho was the first city of many to which God was leading His people in victory. All these nations put together composed the promised land. After Moses died, God reminded Joshua of His oath by saying, "Be strong and courageous, because you will lead these people to inherit the land I swore to their ancestors to give them" (Josh. 1:6).

Then in Joshua 6:2, God gives His word that He would personally hand deliver Jericho over to His people—and give them total victory: "See, I have delivered Jericho into your hands, along with its king and its fighting men." Before He ever gave detailed instructions on how the Israelites would defeat the Jerichoites, He first gave Joshua the direct assurance that He had already delivered them over to Joshua.

You see, when God says He is going to do something—even if that something is in the future—it's as good as done. Even if that something seems absolutely impossible, God will make a way because His promises are guaranteed. Reverend H. G. Salter put it this way: "Every promise is built upon four pillars; God's justice and holiness, which will not suffer Him to deceive; His grace or goodness, which will not suffer Him to forget; His truth, which will not suffer Him to change; His power, which makes Him able to accomplish."[4]

Throughout the Bible, we see a powerful God delivering on His promises to imperfect people and inviting them to participate in His divine plan. God chose Noah to build an ark to keep a remnant alive through the relentless forty-day flood. He chose Esther to save her entire race from a plot to kill them. He chose Jeremiah, Isaiah, Hosea, Amos, and others to prophesy to His people and beckon them to repent. God chose Peter to be the first to take the gospel to the Gentiles, followed by Paul. He chose the woman with the alabaster jar of perfume to teach Jesus' disciples about true worship and devotion. All these were ordinary people like us. God had a special purpose for each of them, and He has a purpose for you and me.

> THROUGHOUT THE BIBLE, WE SEE A POWERFUL GOD DELIVERING ON HIS PROMISES TO IMPERFECT PEOPLE AND INVITING THEM TO PARTICIPATE IN HIS DIVINE PLAN.

NO ACCIDENT

I once heard my friend, Pastor Mike Breaux, preach a sermon in which he related God's plan and purpose to a line in the movie *Forrest Gump*. Toward the end of the film, the protagonist, Forrest Gump, played by Tom Hanks, says, "I don't know if Momma was right or if it's Lieutenant Dan. I don't know if we each have a destiny, or if we're all just floating around accidental-like on a breeze."[5] In response to this, Mike Breaux said this:

> That's the question everybody who ever walks this planet has to come to grips with! Do we just show up accidental-like and float around accidental-like, like a feather on a breeze—or do you and I really have a destiny?
>
> As I look around, I see so many people who tragically have bought into the idea that we just kind of show up and float around accidental-like, like a feather on a breeze. And if that's true, then there really is no destiny. And if there's no destiny, there is no purpose. And if there's no purpose, there's no truth. And if there's no truth, then there's no real right or wrong because it's whatever is right or wrong for you.
>
> In fact, for the past two decades the word that sociologists have used to describe our culture is *whatever*. And I get that. We're taught from a very young age that we've evolved from accidental pond stuff—that we came from nothing and we're going to nothing, so everything else in between would kind of be like, whatever. . . .
>
> But hasn't it been your experience so far in this life that it's simply not true? Don't you have sense that you were put here

on this planet for a purpose? Isn't there something inside you that says, "No, no, no! Man, I didn't show up here accidental-like and I'm not floating around accidental-like, like a feather on a breeze. There's a destiny for me." Well, if you're thinking that, you're right.[6]

Just as God had a destiny in mind for a prostitute named Rahab, He also has a sovereign plan for you. Your life is not an accident. You are called to a higher purpose. One of my favorite passages in all Scripture is found in Jeremiah 29:11, which says, "'For I know the plans I have for you,' declares the LORD, 'plans to prosper you and not to harm you, plans to give you hope and a future.'"

There is a God in heaven who created you, made you, formed you, and knows you. The Bible says God not only knitted you together in your mother's womb (Ps. 139:13), but also prepared good works in advance for you to do (Eph. 2:10). Your heavenly Father had a plan for you in Christ Jesus from before the beginning of time. Take a look at one of the most convincing evidences from Scripture:

> Long before he laid down earth's foundations, he had us in mind, had settled on us as the focus of his love, to be made whole and holy by his love. Long, long ago he decided to adopt us into his family through Jesus Christ. (What pleasure he took in planning this!) He wanted us to enter into the celebration of his lavish gift-giving by the hand of his beloved Son. (Eph. 1:4–6 MSG)

Likewise, God had it in mind to bring Rahab into the grand plan He had for the Israelites. And just as it was no accident that she encountered the two spies on the fateful night described in Joshua chapter 2, it's no accident that you were born or that you've had the experiences you've had in life thus far. Even the trials, hardships, and walls. God has a purpose to bring all these circumstances together for your good and for His glory (Rom. 8:28).

CROSSING THE BRIDGE

Now that you understand that God has a unique plan for you and all humanity, there is an important bridge you must cross today: to decide whether or not you are willing to trust in this plan. This is the proverbial "moment of truth." Every single person must make this decision. Do you believe that God's plan is in your best interest? Will you trust in God's plan for your life and cross over the bridge in obedience, or will you remain on one side of the shore, seeking to handle this problem in your own strength?

Trust is a common theme throughout the Bible, appearing 170 times in the New International Version.[7] Trust is also a vital element of your personal journey to conquer your impossible obstacles, so let's talk about what the word really means. *Trust* is defined as:

- reliance on the integrity, strength, ability, surety, etc., of a person or thing; confidence.
- confident expectation of something; hope.
- confidence in the certainty of future payment for property or goods received; credit: to sell merchandise on trust.
- a person on whom or thing on which one relies: God is my trust.
- the condition of one to whom something has been entrusted.[8]

In whom or what do you put your trust, confident expectation, and hope? Your parents? Your spouse? Money? The government? Your teachers? Your abilities? At the risk of sounding like a downer, I can say with confidence that every single thing under the sun will let you down at some time or another. Parents may disappoint or frustrate you. Spouses are imperfect. Money will run out eventually. Government officials are unreliable. Our own abilities rust as we get older. Even the sun will let you down. It can burn your skin, melt your ice cream, or hide on your wedding day—and someday scientists predict that it will use up all its fuel and burn out altogether.

But God? He is the same yesterday and today and forever (Heb. 13:8). The Lord will never leave or forsake you (Deut. 31:6-8; Ps. 9:10; Heb. 13:5). He alone is "is trustworthy in all he promises and faithful in all he does" (Ps. 145:13).

God's people had to decide whether or not they would put their faith in His proven trustworthiness and faithfulness when He gave them seemingly nonsensical instructions to march around the walls of Jericho for seven days in order to bring about the city's destruction (Josh. 6:2–5). Joshua and the Israelites obeyed Him because they trusted Him. As a result, they were victorious.

Whenever we put our trust in someone or something, it is evidenced by a subsequent action. If you trust your parents, you will listen to them when they tell you not to cross the street until you've looked both ways for oncoming cars. If you trust your spouse, you're not going to follow him or her around town to spy on his or her every move out of fear of infidelity. If you trust in money, you will place your identity and security in how much money you can make, and you will probably worry about your bills and choose to work excessive hours rather than spending time with your family. If you trust in your own abilities, you might become devastated if you make a mistake at your job or suffer an injury on the athletic field.

If you trust in God you will obey His commands, which are found in His Word. It is a common saying that "B. I. B. L. E." stands for "Basic Instructions Before Leaving Earth," and putting your trust in God means that you will follow these instructions—just as Joshua, the Israelites, and countless faithful others have done. You will never go wrong by trusting God. Today, commit to memory Proverbs 3:5–6, which encourages us in this way:

> Trust in the LORD with all your heart
>   and lean not on your own understanding;
> in all your ways acknowledge him,
>   and he will make your paths straight.

Oh, how comforting it is to rely upon a God who has the power to make our paths straight. It doesn't matter if your path has been winding and crooked all this time. All you have to do is trust in the Lord and He will correct your course with truth and righteousness. He will level it with love and plant security along its edges. He will remove from your path the weeds of confusion and fear.

It's up to you and it's up to me to accept that He has a plan for our lives. And when we do, oh, what an adventure it will be! As Charles H. Spurgeon once wrote, "God has great things in store for His people; they ought to have large expectations."[9]

When Rahab made a deal with the Israelite spies, the course of her life changed forever. Though she once was stuck in the monotony of sin and an uneventful existence, she made a choice to trust in Yahweh, the God of the Israelites, for the salvation of her entire family—and a brand-new life. Because of Rahab's faith, she became involved in the Lord's mighty plan, the repercussions of which would last far beyond this single event, as we will see later.

FEAR NOT

In order to fully grasp what it means to trust in God's plan, we must spend a few moments examining fear, which is the opposite of trust. I believe fear stems from a lack of trust in the Lord's faithfulness, love, and ability to provide. If you and I trusted in these unwavering qualities of our ever-present God, we would never entertain a single fear.

And yet, everyone in the world fears the exact same thing: losing. Think about what scares you the most. What keeps you awake at night, wrestling with worry? Whether it's your health or the health of a loved one, worries about school or your career, the fear of death or not having enough money, we all fear losing something that we value.

If your biggest source of anxiety right now is failing at a critical project at work, isn't the root of that fear the risk of losing your reputation as a competent worker, and possibly losing your job? And if you lost your job, you would lose your source of income, which would cause you to lose your house, car, and your other possessions—thereby making you lose your sense of security. Then you wouldn't be able to provide for your spouse and your children and maybe you would lose them too. If you're afraid to share your faith with a close friend, isn't it because you're afraid that offending him or her will cause you to lose that friendship?

You see, the real issue is not that we're afraid of failing or sharing our faith. Each issue can be boiled down to determine what the deeper fear actually is. And in every instance, what we fear is loss. We all fear having the most important thing in our lives taken away from us—our health, security, safety, money, relationships, property, or freedom. These are all valid concerns, but they wilt and wither in the light of God's greatness and His promises.

Lloyd Ogilvie, former chaplain of the United States Senate, once noted that there are 366 passages in the Bible that direct us not to worry or fear. That's one encouraging verse for every day of the year, including leap years![10] For example, every believer would be wise to commit Psalm 27:1 to memory. It's a powerful verse as we reflect on the keys to conquering our impossible enemies:

> The LORD is my light and my salvation—
> whom shall I fear?
> The LORD is the stronghold of my life—
> of whom shall I be afraid?

I love Isaiah 41:10, in which our heavenly Father said, "So do not fear, for I am with you; do not be dismayed, for I am your God. I will strengthen you and help you; I will uphold you with my righteous right hand."

Of course, there are hundreds of other verses in the Bible that admonish us not to fear besides the two that I highlighted above. I think the Word is filled with so many of these bold reminders because God knew that His beloved children would easily lose sight of the fact that He is in control. John Ortberg, in his book *If You Want to Walk on Water, You've Got to Get Out of the Boat*, discussed a greater reason:

The single command in Scripture that occurs more often than any other—God's most frequently repeated instruction—is formulated in two words:

Fear not.

Do not be afraid. Be strong and courageous. You can trust me. Fear not.

Why does God command us not to fear?

Fear does not seem like the most serious vice in the world. It never made the list of the Seven Deadly Sins. No one ever receives church discipline for being afraid. So why does God tell human beings to stop being afraid more often than he tells them anything else?

My hunch is that the reason God says "Fear not" so much is *not* that he wants us to be spared emotional discomfort. In fact, usually he says it to get people to do something that is going to lead them into greater fear anyway.

I think God says "fear not" so often because fear is the number one reason human beings are tempted to avoid doing what God asks them to do.[11]

Imagine if Joshua had stood beneath the shadow of the giant walls of Jericho and succumbed to fear rather than belief in the Lord's plan. Do you think the Israelites would have been prevented from inheriting the promised land? I don't. I think God would have used some other trustworthy person to fulfill His purpose. We learn from scriptures like Esther 4:14, Proverbs 21:30, Isaiah 6:8, and Isaiah 14:27 that God's plans always will succeed, and that He uses willing and trusting people to bring His plans to fruition. Joshua's fears could have robbed him of the joy of being a part of God's plan, but they would not have thwarted God's plans.

William Shakespeare once wrote, "Our doubts are traitors, and make us lose the good we oft might win by fearing to attempt."[12] This is a good way to think about our fears in light of trusting God's plan. Our fears will betray us rather than help us. It doesn't always feel that way because fear has a nasty way of convincing us that it's only looking out for our best interests in order to spare us from harm or pain.

But fear rarely does anything but immobilize us from doing what God has purposed for us. Fear is our enemy. It sabotages our good intentions and paralyzes us from doing what the Lord has called us to do. How many times have you felt the Spirit's call to stand for what is right, share the gospel with someone, or go on a mission trip? And how many times have you silenced that voice because you were afraid of what might happen?

Here's the truth: we're all afraid. But if we don't take a leap of faith, we'll just stand at the precipice and wonder what might have been had we leapt. Still need an extra ounce of courage? Try love. We discover in the Word of God that love is the secret weapon for combatting fear. Take a look at 1 John 4:18: "There is no fear in love. But perfect love drives out fear." As you stand before your seemingly impossible obstacles, recall the love of God. By grasping its purity, perfection, and strength, you will be able to cast aside your fears and be reminded to trust in the One who always keeps your best interests at heart.

> FEAR RARELY DOES ANYTHING BUT IMMOBILIZE US FROM DOING WHAT GOD HAS PURPOSED FOR US. FEAR IS OUR ENEMY. IT SABOTAGES OUR GOOD INTENTIONS AND PARALYZES US FROM DOING WHAT THE LORD HAS CALLED US TO DO.

HOW WILL I KNOW?

So you've realized that God indeed has a unique plan for you and the entire world, and you've made a decision to trust this plan. Now you may find yourself wondering, *How will I know what God's plan is for my life exactly?* Good question.

God reveals His plan to us in many, many ways. Often people live as though God never speaks to them, but God speaks to us in a thousand ways. He communicates His plan to us through the Bible. By reading the Word, we discover that the Lord's will involves you and me:

- fleeing from sin (Matt. 4:17);
- living a holy life (1 Peter 1:16);
- forgiving those who have sinned against us (Matt. 6:14);
- loving others (Luke 10:27);
- growing in the knowledge of the truth (Col. 1:10);
- sharing our faith in the gospel (Matt. 28:19);
- taking care of widows and orphans (James 1:27);
- feeding the hungry and clothing the needy (Matt. 25:34–40); and
- seeking justice for the oppressed (Isa. 1:17).

The Lord also communicates His plan to us through the Holy Spirit, counsel from other Christians, lessons from experiences and failures, lessons we learn from watching others who've gone before us, every sunset, every rainbow, every hospital, every siren, every wave, every star. God trying to speak to you, trying to get your attention, trying to share His will with you. And, ultimately, God's gift of His only Son—Jesus—was an attempt to speak to you, to communicate His plan and His love for you.

Sometimes God will speak to you in a small but audible voice that resonates within your heart. Throughout the Bible, we see how the Lord spoke directly to various people. He gave very specific information to Adam and Eve, Noah, Abraham, Isaac, Jacob, Moses, Joshua, the prophets, and Jesus Christ. His voice was heard from heaven at Jesus' baptism, announcing His love for and pleasure in His one and only Son (Matt. 3:16–17).

But we may not always hear from God so explicitly. I understand that this can be problematic for a world full of people searching for answers to important questions. As a pastor I am often asked, "How do I know what God's plan is for my life?" I have come to understand that this question generally can be translated to mean something more definitive, such as, "Where should I go to college?" "What should I do for a living?" "Whom should I marry?" "How do I solve this problem?" "What should I do in this particular situation?" or "How do I get out of this bad predicament?"

It's our human nature to want to know the entire game plan for our lives—*right now*. But our job simply is to focus on one day at a time. That's what Jesus told us to do, after all. He said in Matthew 6:34, "Therefore do not worry about tomorrow, for tomorrow will worry about itself. Each day has enough trouble of its own."

As the Israelites marched around the walls of Jericho and followed God's seven-day plan, they had no choice but to take it one step at a time and one day at a time. Isn't that what our Christian walk is all about? How blessed we would be if our only concern each day was trusting God, seeking Him daily, and walking by faith.

Try this for a week: When you wake up each morning—before you leave your bed and before your feet touch the floor—pray earnestly, "Lord, what do you want me to do today?" Then spend a few minutes with your eyes closed, listening for the voice of God.

Try that for seven days and see how faithful God is to answer you when you take the time to ask and to listen. He will let you know exactly what He wants you to do each day. It could be as general as "I want you to be a good steward of your time and talent at work today." Or as specific as "Call this person and tell them you love them," or "Forgive," or "Stop by the coffee shop before work and buy breakfast for the homeless man you see every day."

God has a plan, and He desires to share this plan with you. Ask Him. Take the time to listen. Wait for Him. If you don't hear an answer right away, keep asking, seeking, and knocking until you hear from the Lord (Luke 11:9). You will be surprised by a whole new agenda—the Lord's agenda—that will be revealed to you in time.

WHEN THE PLAN DOESN'T MAKE SENSE

There will come a time in your life when God's plan is revealed to you, but it may not make sense to you. When He asked the Israelites to march around a wall for seven days, it seemed like a simple request, but let's face it—it wasn't exactly a conventional military strategy. Usually the idea is to sneak up on one's enemy with a surprise attack. But instead, God basically instructed the Israelites to announce their arrival with a parade. He said to Joshua:

> March around the city once with all the armed men. Do this
> for six days. Have seven priests carry trumpets of rams' horns
> in front of the ark. On the seventh day, march around the city
> seven times, with the priests blowing the trumpets. When you
> hear them sound a long blast on the trumpets, have the whole

army give a loud shout; then the wall of the city will collapse
and the army will go up, everyone straight in. (Josh. 6:3–5)

God's plan was the exact opposite of what was typical in a military advance. Rather than approaching Jericho quickly, quietly, and unannounced, the Israelites were to spend seven days walking around the city in plain view of the citizens inside the city. On the last day, they were supposed to make a big ol' ruckus with trumpets and horns and shouting, giving the Jerichoites a total of thirteen warnings (six circuits around the walls the first six days and seven circuits around the walls on the seventh day) that they were going to attack. That's a little odd, don't you think?

And while the Lord may have been specific about *what* He wanted Joshua and the Israelites to do, He was quite vague about *how* He was going to accomplish His plan through their actions. But notice that the Bible doesn't say that God's people questioned His plan. When Joshua conveyed the atypical plan to the people, they didn't say, "Are you joshing us, Joshua?" Instead of balking at the strange directive, Joshua 6:8 tells us that they "went forward." They trusted God and obeyed His command.

It makes me think of the relationships we had with our parents when we were children or teenagers. Do you remember your mom or dad asking you to do something that seemed really dumb to you at the time? Perhaps it was a simple task you didn't think was necessary or a chore they wanted done in a particular way. You usually responded with protests, questions, bargaining, and eye rolling. Hopefully as you've gotten older, you have been able to look back and recognize the wisdom in your parents' requests, but it's difficult to see it when you're young.

When I was a child, I loved to play baseball. Sometimes I was the first baseman; sometimes I was an outfielder, but the position I played primarily was the pitcher. I was the tall, skinny kid on the pitcher's mound, enjoying the thrill of trying to throw strikes. The Little League I belonged to usually had games on Wednesday nights. I had to tell my coach, even before the season started, that I also had church on Wednesday nights. Actually, we had church on Sunday mornings, Sunday nights, *and* Wednesday nights, and my parents expected me to be there without fail. It didn't matter if I was pitching in the game or not.

The Wednesday night Bible study, which my dad taught, would start at 7:15 p.m. sharp and end at 8:00 p.m. Many times I would have a shutout going in a game, or it would be later in the innings, but right around 7:00 p.m., I'd look over and my dad would be there in the car, and I would have to walk off the pitcher's mound. It didn't matter what the score was, how big of a lead we had, or how close of a game it was. I had to walk off the pitcher's mound during the game, take my glove off, take my hat off, get in the car, and go to church. It was extremely embarrassing—I think I still might be suffering from it to this day!

But my dad, bless his heart, was trying to teach his son something: "When it comes time for church, son, you need to be in church, because spiritual matters are far more important than physical matters." As mortifying as it may have been to me at the time, this awkward lesson would be instrumental in God's plan for my life—to become a preacher who has deep convictions about the importance of attending church, gathering together with the body of believers, and cherishing the Word of God.

And now that I have children of my own, I have a great appreciation for my parents and the challenge of child rearing in a godly manner. If I ask my son or one of my daughters to do something, it may be because I'm attempting to teach him or her how to be a respectful, responsible, God-fearing adult—which is no easy feat in the culture in which we live. I may be trying to instill a strong work ethic into my children. If I ask them to do something that seems foolish, it might be because there's more to it than meets the eye, but I don't have time to explain myself.

Whatever my reasoning may be, my hope is that my children will trust me and do what I ask because they know I love them and have their best interests at heart. It's the same in our relationship with God. As His children, we would do well to trust Him because His ways are not our ways, and His thoughts are higher than our thoughts (Isa. 55:8–9). We know He loves us and always is working all things together for our good as part of His sovereign plan (Rom. 8:28–29).

But know this: whenever we operate out of our faith in God's plan, our actions may cause people to look at us and think we are foolish. It appears foolish to the world that a kid would have to walk off the pitcher's mound in the middle of a game in order to go to church. Christians look foolish when we give 10 percent of our incomes to the work of the Lord in accordance with Malachi 3:8–10. It seems silly to the world that we obey the simple command of baptism, even though Jesus instructed every single believer to do so in Matthew 28:19. It looks foolish when a young believer abstains from sex until he or she gets married in obedience to the Word of God (Rom. 13:13; 1 Cor. 6:18). It looks foolish that Christians believe Jesus is alive and that He is coming again in glory to judge the living and the dead, but as 1 Corinthians 1:18 says, "The message of the cross is foolishness to those who are perishing, but to us who are being saved it is the power of God."

OUR RESPONSE TO ANY TASK THE LORD ASKS US TO DO—HOWEVER SIMPLE OR SEEMINGLY SILLY—REVEALS THE COMMITMENT OF OUR HEARTS.

It must have seemed terribly foolish when Naaman, the commander of King Aram's army, was told to wash seven times in the muddy waters of the Jordan River to be cleansed of his leprosy in 2 Kings 5. I'm sure that many people said, "Naaman, that is crazy. You can't get rid of leprosy by dipping in water—let alone dirty water!" Naaman himself was reluctant and skeptical. Yet when he came out of the water after the seventh time, the Bible said that his skin "was restored and became clean like that of a young boy" (2 Kings 5:14).

God's plan is unique and may not always make sense. When He asks us to do something we don't understand, He compels us to decide whether or not we fully trust Him. Our response to any task the Lord asks us to do—however simple or seemingly silly— reveals the commitment of our hearts.

God asked His people simply to walk around the city of Jericho for seven days in order to see its defeat. For the second day in a row, nothing happened. They simply walked. It's possible that those inside the city of Jericho who were looking down at the Israelites from the top of the wall began to mock the people of God. We know that the Jerichoites were afraid of the Israelites at first, but it's possible that their fear turned to jeering by the second or third day as they observed God's people engaging in a task that seemed so senseless.

Even if the men and women of Jericho didn't resort to ridicule, at some point during the day, the Israelites may have been thinking, *This is crazy! We look like idiots!* Did you know that the word *idiot* actually appears in the Bible? It's true. In Acts 4, Peter and John are put into prison in Jerusalem for telling others about Jesus Christ. When they are brought before the rulers, elders, and teachers of the law the next day, Peter is filled with the Holy Spirit and boldly shares the message of salvation with them. Acts 4:13 tells what happened next: "When they saw the courage of Peter and John and realized that they were unschooled, ordinary men, they were astonished and they took note that these men had been with Jesus." The Greek word for "unschooled" is *idiōtēs*.[13] It's where we get the English word *idiot*. The Bible says that Peter and John may have looked like idiots, but because of their faith and courage, the rulers, elders, and teachers of the law were taken aback and took note that they had been with Jesus.

As Christians, we should make it evident by our words and our deeds that we, too, have been with Jesus. It doesn't matter if you look foolish to everyone else. Our Lord Jesus Christ wasn't spared from ridicule as He hung on a cross while skeptics and fickle followers mocked and spat at Him—just as Psalm 22 foretold. Jesus and the apostles experienced suffering and scorn, and so will every person who chooses to serve the Lord, according to the Bible (2 Tim. 3:12). Despite earthly hardships and obstacles, you and I will be used for the glory of God and have the honor of being a part of His extraordinary plan.

DECISION TIME

J. C. Watts once said, "Character is doing the right thing when nobody's looking."[14] I agree with that. But sometimes strong character is revealed when you do the right thing when everyone *is* looking. It's following the Lord despite the stares and jokes of others who don't believe. It's obeying God's commands when everyone else is not.

Despite how you may look to others, you have to say, "I'm going to choose to trust in God's plan anyway." You have to wake up every day and decide to walk according to His plan, for your sole concern as a Christian should be to please God, not man (Gal. 1:10). Why is this decision important in your quest to see the walls fall down in your personal Jericho? Because failing to trust God in the little things will prevent you from having ultimate victory. Take a careful look at what God said to His people back in Deuteronomy 30:11–16; they are important words for every believer:

> Now what I am commanding you today is not too difficult for you or beyond your reach. It is not up in heaven, so that you have to ask, "Who will ascend into heaven to get it and proclaim it to us so we may obey it?" Nor is it beyond the sea, so that you have to ask, "Who will cross the sea to get it and proclaim it to us so we may obey it?" No, the word is very near you; it is in your mouth and in your heart so you may obey it.
>
> See, I set before you today life and prosperity, death and destruction. For I command you today to love the LORD your God, to walk in obedience to him, and to keep his commands, decrees and laws; then you will live and increase, and the LORD your God will bless you in the land you are entering to possess.

The simple instructions the Lord gives us to follow every day are not hard to understand, nor are they hard to do. Sometimes God gives us just a little bit of information and expects us to trust Him because "we walk by faith, not by sight" (2 Cor. 5:7 NKJV).

We may not always know what God is going to do; we just know He is going to do *something*. That's the genius of this entire story— all the children of Israel did was walk, but every step was a step of faith. Soon, those steps would lead to victory.

———⟶———

Rahab and her family huddled close together in front of the window as they watched the walls of Jericho crumble like a stale flatbread in the hands of a toddler. The ground rumbled from the impact. Then, loud footsteps marched purposefully toward their home. As the front door flung open, Rahab's mother and sisters screamed in unison.

It was the two spies from a few days ago. Rahab held her breath. Were they here to take her and her family into captivity, or would they honor the oath they had made to her?

"Hurry!" said the stouter of the two young men. "We have to go now."

Rahab let out a sigh of relief and ushered her family to the door as the second spy stood watch. Her little brother, Yassib, stood frozen in his tracks. Screams could be heard from outside along with the crackling sound of wood being consumed by fire. The smell of smoke wafted into Rahab's house.

The first spy knelt down to Yassib's eye level and tapped the necklace he had given the boy, which hovered over his heart. "Take courage," he told Yassib. "We're going to get you out of here safely, and we're going to a better place."

Yassib snapped out of his daze and dashed out the door to join his family. Then the spies brought Rahab out of

Jericho—along with her father, mother, brothers, sisters, and all who belonged to her—and placed them in a spot outside the camp of Israel.

"Then they burned the whole city and everything in it, but they put the silver and gold and the articles of bronze and iron into the treasury of the LORD's house. But Joshua spared Rahab the prostitute, with her family and all who belonged to her, because she hid the men Joshua had sent as spies to Jericho—and she lives among the Israelites to this day."[15]

⤙⤚

In an instant, Rahab's destiny changed forever. No longer would she be known as "Rahab the prostitute." Instead, she is counted among the righteous people of faith throughout the Bible (Heb. 11:31; James 2:25). And it gets even better. What Rahab did for the two Israelite spies was important, yes. But God had bigger plans for Rahab than that simple moment in time.

Ephesians 2:13–15 reveals that it was God's purpose from the beginning to make one family of faith through both Jews and Gentiles and to reconcile all people to Him through Jesus Christ. This was the Lord's overarching plan, and He used Rahab to accomplish it. In Matthew 1:5, we find Rahab included in the long and detailed genealogy that brought our Savior into the world. What an immense honor to be used for the glory of God!

Rahab's story shows us that the Lord can use and involve anyone in His magnificent purposes. No matter your past, the mistakes you've made, or how undervalued you might be in the eyes of other people; in God's eyes, your potential is limitless. He has a unique plan for you. Trust Him and you will be one big step closer to victory.

A PRAYER FOR TODAY

Dear Lord, Thank you that no matter my past, my credentials or qualifications, or lack thereof, You have a unique plan for me. Your Word says in Jeremiah 29:11 that You wish to prosper and not to harm me, to give me hope and a future. I'm so glad You are faithful to deliver on Your promises. Father, I have decided to put my trust in Your plan. No more wavering. No more worrying. No more fear. Will you please reveal Your specific plan for this season in my life through Your Word, Your Spirit, wise and godly counsel, and prayer? And please help me to obey even when Your plan may not make sense to me. In Jesus' name I pray, amen.

MAKE IT A HOLY EXERCISE

See the supernatural in all situations.

Aryeh crouched down, studying the detailed sketch of the walls of Jericho he had drawn in the moist sand. As a commander in the Israelite army, second only to Joshua, everyone would be counting on him for a bold strategy for penetrating this impregnable fortress. Brow furrowed from deep concentration, Aryeh contemplated how he and his men would surmount the first barrier: a mud-brick wall that was at least seventeen cubits high and sat *on top* of a retaining wall that was another ten cubits high. If—and it was a very big "if"—they somehow were able to conquer this obstacle, they would be met by a steep embankment leading up to the plateau upon which the formidable city was built. At the crest of this embankment stood another tall, mud-brick wall that was thirty-one cubits above ground level.[1]

Turning to Seth, who had been stooped next to him quietly, Aryeh said, "Tell me about the gates of the second wall."

"They're securely barred, sir," Seth replied solemnly. "Most likely with the finest cedar from Lebanon. It would be very difficult to break through. An impossibility."

Seth was right. Two impenetrable and insurmountable walls composed of tightly stacked mud-brick stones that could weigh as much as ten heavy talents each, with a steep embankment in between them.[2] It was a fool's mission.

A man of few words, Aryeh let out a low growl. Seth was used to hearing this sound whenever the commander was annoyed or frustrated. Aryeh's name meant "lion" in Hebrew, and much like the cunning beast, he was a clever military strategist who was known to pounce on an opportunity with fierce precision. The walls of Jericho, however, were a challenge like no other.

The commander stood and collected his thoughts. He had an idea. It would be a long shot at best, but at least the Israelite army could attempt it—and pray to God that the plan would work. So with Seth following behind, Aryeh stalked through the camp until he found Joshua. He was talking among the Levite priests in an animated manner that Aryeh found to be quite perplexing.

Seeing the two faithful warriors approaching, Joshua excused himself from the company of the priests. "Hello, Aryeh! Hello, Seth!" Joshua welcomed them.

This was a more confident Joshua than Aryeh had seen just a few days ago. Some said he had heard the voice of God.

"Sir, I have something to show you," Aryeh told Joshua in his typical stoic manner.

He led Joshua and Seth back to the area of sand in which he had sketched the walls of their enemy's fortress.

"Infiltrating the city of Jericho presents us with a series of grave obstacles, sir," Aryeh said. "I've never seen such a well-protected city in all my years serving the army of Israel." He went on to explain the dimensions of the two walls, the weight of the stones, and the arduous hill leading up to where the bastion of Jericho was perched.

"It's an almost futile mission," Aryeh continued. "An unattainable goal. However, I can send teams of soldiers out to the first wall at night, to search every stone for some kind of breach in the structure. We might be able to find something, but even if we get past the first wall and make it up the hill without being attacked, we still have a second wall to face, and its gates are securely barred."

"Aryeh—" Joshua interjected, but the commander must not have heard him.

"Now, we do have a psychological advantage, if you will," Aryeh said. "It is said that the entire city is melting in fear because of us. Their armed men may be hiding within the city, leaving the battlements unmanned."

"Aryeh—" Joshua tried once more.

"Or, we can dig a large tunnel beneath the wall. It might take some time but I believe—"

"Aryeh, Aryeh," Joshua reiterated, finally causing the commander to pause. "Thank you for your very thorough analysis of the challenge before us."

"Sir?" Aryeh was truly befuddled.

"You've done good work and made an excellent proposal," Joshua said. "However, we will neither search for a breach in the wall nor dig a tunnel beneath it, for the Lord God Almighty has given us *His* plan for conquering the city of Jericho."

Joshua shared with Aryeh and Seth how the word of the

Lord had come to him, instructing him simply to march around the walls of the city with the priests and armed men once a day for six days. God told him to have seven priests carry trumpets made of rams' horns in front of the ark. Then, on the seventh day, they were to march around the city seven times with the priests blowing the trumpets. When they heard the last long blast, the entire army would give a loud shout, and the walls of the city would collapse before them.

"God Himself has pronounced that He has delivered Jericho into our hands," said Joshua.

A low growl emerged from deep inside the commander's throat. Seth took a quick step backward as Aryeh suddenly kicked the ground and sent a heap of sand cascading forth to cover the meticulous map he had drawn. It was ruined, but it didn't matter.

"I'm sorry, commander," Joshua replied. "This is what I was discussing with the priests back at the camp. I was very eager to share this information with you as well, but you seemed determined to show me what you had devised."

"This strategy makes no sense!" Aryeh roared. "We're going to walk around a wall for seven days in plain sight of our enemies. And on the last day, we're supposed to holler and shout like unruly children and expect the walls to come tumbling down for us? Not only are we going to look like fools, but we'll also be remembered as fools for the rest of our lives!"

"It is not my plan, but the Lord's," Joshua replied. "And when you think about it, it makes perfect sense. We'll have the front guard marching just ahead of the priests, followed by the ark of the covenant, followed by the rear guard. Do you know what that means, Aryeh?"

"No," Aryeh muttered.

"Since God's presence dwells within the ark of the covenant and the ark of the covenant will be in the center of the procession," Joshua explained, "it means that Yahweh Himself will be at the center of what we are doing. It is His rightful place."

Aryeh softened. The plan may not have made sense to him militarily, but he knew that from a spiritual standpoint, God's divine power would be with the Israelites if they placed His holy ark in the middle of their cavalcade. After all, the Lord often operated in ways that did not make sense to the commander, but they were always sure and effective. God used a pillar of cloud to guide the Israelites by day and a pillar of fire to guide and give them light at night as they escaped Egypt.[3] He divided the Red Sea to allow His people to cross through it and made the waters engulf the best of Pharaoh's army.[4] The Lord provided bread from the sky and quail each day for the Israelites to eat in the midst of a barren desert.[5] He caused water to pour from a rock in Rephidim when the people were thirsty.[6] What's more, His ark—His presence—was always in the direct center of their everyday lives in the camp, so this special mission should be no different.

Aryeh did not fully understand how the plan would work, but his remembrance of God's miracles and his commitment to Joshua's army far outweighed his confusion. Finally he spoke.

"You give the order to the armed men," Aryeh said, "and we will do as you have said, just as the Lord has commanded to do."

For the casual Bible reader, there is a seemingly small detail within God's instructions that easily can be overlooked: the positioning of seven priests with seven trumpets and the ark of the covenant in the middle of the procession of the Israelite army. But this specification reveals a critical component in our journey to conquering our impossible obstacles. Whenever we endeavor to do something, whether it's a small task or a huge venture, there is a spiritual element that we must recognize and embrace. Intelligence is important, strategy is significant, and might is meaningful. However, if we are to be successful in any area of life, it's imperative that we put God at the center of our plans—seeking Him in all that we do, and surrendering to Him every step of the way. If we desire to cause the walls to come tumbling down in a hopeless situation, we must make it a *holy exercise.*

When God said to Joshua, "See, I have delivered Jericho into your hands, along with its king and its fighting men. March around the city once with all the armed men. Do this for six days" (Josh. 6:2–3), I can imagine a gung ho Joshua ready to spring into action with his courageous army, weapons in hand. But then God continued, "Have seven priests carry trumpets of rams' horns in front of the ark. On the seventh day, march around the city seven times, with the priests blowing the trumpets" (v. 4).

Cue the record-scratch sound effect. "Uh, what's that You say, Lord?"

After hearing this unusual assignment, it would be tempting for Joshua to think, *Priests? A battle is no place for priests. We need lean, mean, well-trained, battlefield-tested soldiers—not holy men in long robes. And why would we bring the ark of the covenant into this tactical mission? We need useful weapons, not a sacred box!* But as anyone who walks closely with the Lord and has seen miracle after miracle firsthand, Joshua knew that the battle was more of a spiritual matter than a physical one.

The apostle Paul wrote in Ephesians 6:12, "For our struggle is not against flesh and blood, but against the rulers,

YOUR CURRENT PROBLEM IS NOT GOING TO BE SOLVED WITH YOUR OWN STRENGTH, MONEY, GOOD LOOKS, LUCK, CLEVERNESS, OR CUNNING— IT WILL ONLY BE SOLVED WHEN YOU MAKE IT A HOLY EXERCISE BY DRAWING GOD INTO THE EQUATION.

against the authorities, against the powers of this dark world and against the spiritual forces of evil in the heavenly realms." This means that no matter how much your problems may seem to be tied to this world (your career issues or finances) or to a person (trouble with a spouse or a rebellious child), it's really a spiritual battle that you are facing.

When Jesus' disciples could not drive out an evil spirit that had possessed a young boy, they asked the Lord why they had been unsuccessful. Jesus said, "This kind can come out by nothing but prayer and fasting" (Mark 9:29 NKJV). Rather than relying upon their own knowledge or power, the disciples needed to make their battle a holy exercise by engaging in prayer and fasting, which are two paramount spiritual disciplines. Likewise, your current problem is not going to be solved with your own strength, money, good looks, luck, cleverness, or cunning—it will only be solved when you make it a holy exercise by drawing God into the equation.

ME, HOLY?

When you think of the word *holy*, what comes to mind? Priests in white robes praying in a chapel by candlelight? Monks meditating in the sacred mountains of China? Angels strumming harps in the heavens above? I'm guessing the first thing you thought of was not a wooden box.

But to serve as a visual reminder of His holy nature, God instructed Moses to supervise the building of the ark of the covenant—a rectangular chest made of acacia wood and overlaid with gold. It housed the tablets of stone upon which the Ten Commandments were inscribed, and it symbolized the very presence of God with the Israelites (Lev. 16:2). Located behind a curtain inside the most holy place within the tabernacle tent, the ark of the covenant was where God met with Moses and gave him His commands for the people (Ex. 25:22).

No other person except the high priest could enter the most holy place and approach the ark of the covenant—and that was only after he had gone through ceremonial cleansing. If anyone broke the rules God set forth concerning the ark, he or she would die (Lev. 16:2; 2 Sam. 6:7). Whenever the ark was moved, the priests had to cover it with several layers of cloth and animal skins to protect others from seeing it (Num. 4:5–6). Everyone had to stay at least three thousand feet away from the ark while the priests carried it (Josh. 3:4). That's more than a half-mile! It is unclear from Joshua chapter 6 whether the soldiers who composed the front and rear guards of the ark in the procession around Jericho had to stay this far away from the ark, but it was very possible.

Now you may be questioning, *Why were there so many rules concerning the ark of the covenant? And isn't it a bit extreme that someone would* die *if he or she disobeyed these rules?* It's difficult for those of us who are not well versed in the culture and religious practices of Judaism to understand the serious nature of God's holiness. He is wholly set apart from everything that exists, and His righteousness surpasses our comprehension. He is divine. He is perfect. Darkness flees at even the smallest glimpse of His glorious presence. God is holy, and there is no other appropriate response toward His holiness than our total and utter reverence.

When the prophet Isaiah had a spectacular vision of God seated on an exalted throne in Isaiah 6:1–7, winged celestial beings flew above Him and chanted, "Holy, holy, holy is the Lord Almighty; the whole earth is full of his glory." The Bible says that at the sound of their voices, the doorposts and thresholds shook and the temple of the Lord filled with smoke. Look at Isaiah's response:

> "Woe to me!" I cried. "I am ruined! For I am a man of unclean lips, and I live among a people of unclean lips, and my eyes have seen the King, the Lord Almighty."
>
> Then one of the seraphim flew to me with a live coal in his hand, which he had taken with tongs from the altar. With it he touched my mouth and said, "See, this has touched your lips; your guilt is taken away and your sin atoned for." (vv. 5–7)

Even Isaiah, a prophet who feared the Lord, had to be cleansed before entering into His presence. Therefore, anyone other than the ceremonially cleansed high priest who approached the ark of the covenant was an unclean person standing in the presence of an exceedingly holy God who, by His very nature, cannot tolerate wickedness (Ps. 5:4–6). In order to be in the presence of the Lord, we ourselves must become holy.

Holiness may seem unattainable for someone who hasn't been called to be a pastor, priest, nun, elder, deacon, or any other devoted member of the clergy. Jack Hayford wrote:

> The average believer seems to feel threatened by the idea of holiness. He tends to see it as something unapproachable, a demanding standard of life that seems to be well beyond him. Believers tend to define it by "feel" more than by fact, and the feeling seems to be, "Boy, that's way beyond me (although I sure want to try my best!)."
>
> The Holy Spirit desires to bring each of us to complete personhood. This practical pursuit—our partnering with Him as He comes to help—is geared to make us whole or holy. That's what 'holiness' is really about—wholeness. What the Holy Spirit is up to is bringing the *whole* life of Jesus Christ into the *whole* of our personalities so that the *whole* love of God can be relayed to the *whole* world.[7]

God desires for His people, the church, to be holy. He makes this possible through His Son Jesus. From Ephesians 5:26–27, we glean a deeper understanding that holiness involves Christ cleansing the church in order to make her radiant, blameless, and without stain, wrinkle, or blemish. It also involves us daily choosing to obey God's command, for as He said in 1 Peter 1:16, "Be holy, because I am holy." And while God sees believers as completely holy through Christ (Eph. 1:4; 2 Cor. 5:21), we still are called to holy behavior (1 John 2:6).

You wouldn't put on a bright white shirt and a pair of white pants and white shoes and jump around in the mud, would you? No. You would take care to avoid walking near even the smallest of puddles or consuming anything like coffee, chocolate, or spaghetti sauce that would stain your pristine clothing. In the same way, since Christ lives in us and makes us righteous in God's eyes, it is only natural that we would remain pure by avoiding sin and obeying His Word. Psalm 119:9 makes it clear: "How can a young person stay on the path of purity? By living according to your word."

> YOU WEREN'T SAVED SO THAT YOU CAN KEEP ONE FOOT IN THE WORLD AND ONE FOOT IN THE CHURCH; YOU WERE SAVED TO BE *HOLY*.

As a pastor, I often get asked, "Is this a sin?" or, "The Bible doesn't say anything about this, so can I do it?" It's almost as if the person just wants to know how fine a line he or she can walk without getting into trouble biblically. He or she continues to pursue ways to gratify sinful desires rather than to run full-speed from anything that would even be close to displeasing the Lord. The aim of our Christian walk is not to see what we can or cannot get away with; it's to do what is holy and pleasing to God. Let me say it again: you weren't saved so that you can keep one foot in the world and one foot in the church; you were saved to be *holy*.

Holiness is an act of worship you display with your life as you reject sin and fill your spirit with the things of God instead of the things of the world. It involves dedicating every day of your life to love and serve the Lord and others, rather than pursuing selfish gain. What this means to me is that you and I are invited to lean on *His* power to strengthen us as He completes the good work He has started in each of us (Phil. 1:6). To be holy is a command of God, but it is also an invitation to become more and more like the One to whom there is no equal—the One who molds and shapes us in His likeness, if we are willing. It's seeking the Lord in every situation, even when you're in the midst of a struggle or trial.

Now that we have a clearer understanding of what it means to be holy and that holiness is indeed possible for every Christian, we can dive in to how exactly we can turn our battle into a holy exercise. I want to share with you five practical ways that will be keys to your success in seeing the walls fall down in your personal Jericho.

1. VISUALIZE GOD IN THE LINE WITH YOU.

Think about the vantage point of the soldiers who were walking around the walls of Jericho. Put yourself in their sandals for a moment. They're involved in this impossible task, marching in a line around these intimidating walls in a foreign land. Each soldier could probably only see the back of the guy who was marching in front of him, and if he turned around, he would be able to see the guy behind him. As the line curved around the wall, the soldiers in the rear guard might have been able to catch a glimpse of the priests ahead who were carrying the ark of the covenant.

Here's my point: If I were a soldier in that line that day, I'd be thinking, *Okay, there's Eli, my next-door neighbor, in front of me. There's my other neighbor, Gershon. There's David, my wife's brother, behind me. There are the priests up ahead. And there's God! God is in my line. I just gotta keep walking because I'm in the line with* God!

Whether you're walking in the depressed line, or the discouraged line, or the overweight line, or the not-enough-money line, or the sickness line today, visualize God in that line with you and keep walking. When the Lord said over and over again in His Word that He would never leave or forsake you, I'm confident He meant *even* in your deep, personal, and painful struggle. When Jesus said in Matthew 28:20 that He is with you always,

I believe He meant even in the battle. Being able to see God in the trenches with you, lovingly and faithfully at your side, turns your issue into a holy exercise. Your eyes are no longer clouded by discouragement or distractions; they are focused solely on the Lord God Almighty.

I grew up in a church where there was a communion table placed at the front of the sanctuary every Sunday. I don't know why, but my little brain always thought that communion table was about the size the ark of the covenant would have been. The wood was elaborately carved, and there was a nice drape placed over it. On top were the elements of communion, the bread and the juice, which represented the body and the blood of Jesus Christ. When we partook in communion each weekend, it was the holiest moment of the service in our minds. And for us, it represented the presence of God just as the ark of the covenant did for Joshua and the Israelites.

Seeing that communion table each week helped to sustain my focus in church. And when you attend your church—after the entire week has been chaotic or full of heartache, strife, struggle, or pain—you walk into that building, and you feel God's presence there. It's why so many faithful believers come back to church week after week. They know God is going to be there. All the distractions and worries from the week melt away because His presence is so much stronger than any problem we might face.

A man by the name of Don Phillips is a member of Shepherd Church, the congregation I pastor in Los Angeles, California. He produced the Academy Award–winning film *Melvin and Howard*, and was the number one casting director in Hollywood at one time. In fact, he has been called "The Man with the Golden Eye" because of his remarkable ability to recognize a star in the making.

He discovered such notable actors as Sean Penn and Matthew McConaughey and gave them both their first big breaks.

Don sits in the front row in church. It's a pretty large auditorium; I don't know why, but it was a little strange to me that someone with his background would make his way to the front and sit in the first row every weekend. One time I asked him, "Don, why do you always sit in the front row?"

And he said, "Dudley, I decided a long time ago that I wasn't living right and that I needed to get right. I knew I needed to get to church and hear the Word. The reason I sit up front is because I want *no* distractions. I don't want to look around and see who's wearing what. I don't want to see who came in late. I don't want my attention taken away by someone talking. I just want to sit in the very front of the church and have absolutely zero distractions so that I can hear every word from God that is preached."

In our world, and especially in Los Angeles where I live, we are surrounded by so many things that are vying for our attention. God stands alone and will not compete with earthly things for your focus. He wants you to get in line with Him. He wants you to be captivated by Him like Mary, Martha's sister who sat at Jesus' feet listening to His teaching (Luke 10). When your eyes are glued to God, it doesn't matter what problems and issues are abuzz around you because you understand where your victory comes from.

2. PUT GOD IN HIS PROPER PLACE.

Though we often try to solve problems on our own, the reality is that you and I are never going to succeed at anything in our own strength. It may seem as if you're getting ahead in your own power at first. But soon you come against one frustrating obstacle after the other and end up confused and wondering where you went wrong. It reminds me of Psalm 127:1, which maintains, "Unless the LORD builds the house, the builders labor in vain. Unless the LORD watches over the city, the guards stand watch in vain."

Let me put it this way: in order to have victory over your problem, you *must* draw God into this equation. God is the one who is going to bring down the imposing walls in your life, and only when you place Him at the center of your life will you be able to succeed as Joshua and the Israelites did at the battle of Jericho. Just as they positioned the ark of the covenant in the center of their procession, when you make God the focus of everything you do—no matter how menial the task or how daunting the struggle—it causes you to realize that *God* is the source of the victory. Therefore, He gets the credit, not you.

Let's say there were two young men from Jericho peeking over the wall or through a crack in the wall to get a better look at the Israelites who had struck fear into their entire city. What would they see? First, they would see a single echelon of armed men who were marching forward with extraordinary focus. Next, they would see seven priests donned in ornate robes, sounding their trumpets and carrying the poles of some mysterious chest. Could it be the famed ark of the covenant, the rumored source of the Israelites' power? Lastly, they would see another line of armed men making up the rear guard behind the priests and the chest. This would be a very peculiar sight to someone from Jericho. The sight of soldiers advancing is frightening enough, but to see an object in which the presence of an all-powerful God was said to dwell would have taken the intensity up another notch.

Though the Israelites were simply walking, the arcane ark

made it clear to everyone that the Lord God Almighty was there in the midst of them. Sure, the Israelites could have marched around the city of Jericho without the ark, but they would have gone about their mission without the presence of God, and they would have been defeated. Having God in the center of their procession made the monotonous task of walking around the walls a sacred and holy exercise, and it ensured their victory.

How can you put the Lord in His rightful place in your life? A great way to start is by slowing down and acknowledging Him in the stillness and quiet. He declared in Psalm 46:10, "Be still, and know that I am God; I will be exalted among the nations, I will be exalted in the earth." If the Israelites had executed the Lord's plan in a rushed or disorderly manner, it's likely that the presence of God via the ark of the covenant would not have been as obvious to the men and women of Jericho. Similarly, it's difficult for you and I to see God—and for others to see Him at work in us personally—when we are running about our daily tasks like crazy people. But when we slow down, rest, and worship, Christ becomes undeniably evident in our lives.

Another way to put the Lord first is by carving out time to read God's Word every single day. I could dedicate an entire book to the importance of believers reading the Bible 365 days a year. It's a deeply personal time with God in which you are learning and soaking in His will and His truth.

Daily prayer is also vital. Prayer is simply a time to praise God, confess sins, ask for forgiveness, and present your needs and worries to Him. The very act of praying connects God to whatever it is you are praying about—however great or small. If you are praying while you're stranded on the side of the freeway with a flat tire, you're connecting God to that problem. If you're praying about an upcoming job interview, you're connecting the Lord to the possibility of that door opening to you. If you're praying over your children's school, you're connecting God to your children, the other students, the teachers, and the administrators.

On the first day of school every year, my dad would have us kneel on the floor and pray. I thought it was silly at the time, but now I see that it was a holy exercise. You, too, can lead your family in prayer at any time of any day. If you are not sure how to pray, read Matthew 6:5–15 for guidance.

Attending church every weekend—no matter what social plans you might have, no matter what game might be on television that day, no matter how you're feeling—is also key. Your faithfulness in this area is what can make all the difference as you seek victory in your current battle. Consistently gathering together with the body of believers is a natural by-product of your love and commitment to God and your desire to put Him first in your life.

Out of the one hundred and thirty thousand babies born in Los Angeles each year, we usually have only about a hundred parents who come to an annual baby dedication service we have at Shepherd. The parents who choose to participate in the baby dedication service are making a public commitment to raise their children in the Lord's way as we are instructed to do in Proverbs 22:6.

Similarly, there are tens of thousands of people who buy a home each year, but only a few people call me or the other pastors on staff and ask one of us to come over to pray and bless their homes. Before they spend one day decorating, arranging furniture, or eating meals inside their houses, they want to engage in the holy exercise of praying for the Lord's blessing. These families understand that putting God in the center of their lives starts in the home. This leads me to point number three.

3. SEE THAT YOUR HOME IS AS HOLY AS THE CHURCH.

There was a time when my wife and I were having difficulty with our son who was in his early college years and living at home. If you are the parent of a young adult, perhaps you will be able to relate. As your kids get older and are still living at home with you, they begin to make their own decisions—decisions you may not always agree with—and yet you have certain rules in your house that need to be respected and followed. It reminds me of a quote I see on the Internet from time to time that reads: "Teenagers, are you tired of being harassed by your stupid parents? Act now! Move out. Get a job. Pay your own way. Quick—while you still know everything."

One day I went into my son's room and shut the door behind me. I sat down on the floor, which gave me a nonconfrontational position, yet with my back against the door to make it nearly impossible for him to leave. He was sitting at his desk with his back to me and wouldn't look over at me. My son, the apple of my eye, was going out into the world and engaging in the things of the world to various dark degrees. He had been fighting me and did not want to obey the rules my wife and I had set for our home.

I began slowly. "Son," I said, "this is not just about you and me. It's not just about you obeying our rules. On the other side of that wall, you have a sixteen-year-old sister who still is pure of heart. And down the hall you have a mother, and she is sacred. She is a borderline saint. Your job and mine is to heed God's calling as the men of this house to set good examples for them."

My son was silent. Not knowing if I was getting through to him or not, I continued, "Here in our house, we have a kitchen, bedrooms, bathrooms, a roof, a garage, and three crazy dogs in the side yard. Yes, this is a house, but it's also a holy place. There is no difference between the church and this house; they're both the same. In fact, the early church met in people's homes. I'm a pastor at church, at home, and everywhere I go. This house—our house—is just as holy as the church. The church is just as holy as this house.

"And there's one more thing I want you to consider," I said. "Son, in thirty years, I probably will be living at your house. You'll be taking care of me. If and when that happens, I'm going to have to live by *your* rules. I might own ten cats, and you could say the rules of your house are no cats. I would have to decide if I was going to abide by your rules and come live with you."

> MANY OF THE PROBLEMS WE FACE ARE BECAUSE WE HAVEN'T MADE OUR HOMES A HOLY PLACE, ALLOWING THE PRESENCE OF GOD TO DWELL AND REIGN IN OUR HOMES.

Then I suggested, "Why don't we try this for the next eight to ten months? Just live in this house under my rules. Let's make this a holy place. And we won't have any problems."

To his and the Lord's credit, my son did exactly that. He turned his life around and is currently posting daily Bible verses on Instagram to more than a hundred thousand followers.[8]

Many of the problems we face are because we haven't made our homes holy places, allowing the presence of God to dwell and reign in our homes. Many people think, *The holy place is down there at the church.* But when you are a believer in Christ, there is no separation between you and the church. First Corinthians 3:16 makes it plain: "Don't you know that you yourselves are God's temple and that God's Spirit dwells in your midst?" Whether you're walking around or within the walls of your house, the mall, the coffee shop, the auto repair place, or your school, remember that you are a holy vessel that the Lord wants to use for His holy purpose.

4. RECOGNIZE THAT VICTORY OFTEN FOLLOWS HOLINESS.

Another reason why we must strive for holiness is because there is raw power in holiness. You want to have victory in your life. That's good! But one of the critical components that ushers in victory is holiness. Many people don't connect the two, but there is a correlation between men and women committing themselves to holiness and God bringing victory.

We see this principle many times throughout the Bible. For example, in Joshua chapter 3, we see holiness preceding victory when the Israelites camped by the Jordan River before they crossed over it on their way to the promised land:

> Joshua told the people, "Consecrate yourselves, for tomorrow the LORD will do amazing things among you."
>
> Joshua said to the priests, "Take up the ark of the covenant and pass on ahead of the people." So they took it up and went ahead of them.
>
> And the LORD said to Joshua, "Today I will begin to exalt you in the eyes of all Israel, so they may know that I am with you as I was with Moses." (vv. 5–7)

After Joshua and the Israelites consecrated themselves, the Lord stopped the waters from flowing downstream in the river Jordan so that the priests and all the people could cross over. We learned in day 1 of our journey in this book that the Jordan represented a huge obstacle in the Israelites' mission to take possession of the promised land, but after they obeyed God's command to consecrate themselves, God gave them victory.

In 2 Chronicles 29, we see another instance of holiness preceding victory when Hezekiah, the king of Judah, ordered the priests to consecrate themselves and reestablished the service of the temple of the Lord. He purified the temple and renewed the heart of worship among the Israelites as the people gave sacrifices and offerings to God and praised Him. The Bible says, "After all that Hezekiah had so faithfully done, Sennacherib king of Assyria came and invaded Judah" (2 Chron. 32:1). Hezekiah may have been thinking, *Wait a minute, Lord; we consecrated ourselves before You, so why is this trouble coming upon us?* But look at what God did next: He sent an angel to annihilate the Assyrian army and saved Hezekiah and the people of Jerusalem (vv. 21–22).

Think of consecration as purifying oneself, getting rid of sin, and devoting oneself to the work of the Lord. It's not just cleaning the outside. It's an inward process of purification, making sure your heart is right before God.

I've joked with people about how my wife, Renee, will go to the store to buy some groceries and come back with one loaf of bread and three gallons of bleach. One of her favorite pastimes is disinfecting the entire house with bleach, because she's a neat freak. Because of that powerful smell, my eyes constantly water when I'm in my house. Renee is an amazing woman, and having a clean house is a good problem to have. But while bleach is effective at sterilizing our homes, all the bleach in the world could not clean a person on the inside.

In order to cleanse our souls, we must make a choice to purify our hearts before God each and every day. As Psalm 139:23–24 says, it's allowing God to search us and know our hearts; to test us and know our anxious thoughts; to see if there is any offensive way in us and lead us in the everlasting way. Whenever you set your heart and mind upon holiness before the Lord, you invite His blessings upon your life and pave the way for victory over the challenges you are facing.

It's quite possible that the victory God's people were about to experience in Jericho had less to do with the defeat of the Jerichoites and more to do with the holiness of the Israelites. People have been aware of this story for thousands of years, and they've probably only seen this as part of God's plan for the Israelites to conquer and inherit the promised land. But what if His ultimate purpose was actually to purify His people through the experience? After all, this is often His purpose in the struggles you and I endure. We yearn impatiently for victory, but there is an important cleansing process God is trying to accomplish within us.

For the Israelites, the very positioning of the priests and the ark of the covenant in the middle of the army was a call to cleansing. The sacred ark was normally hidden within the Holy of Holies in the tabernacle tent. It would have been quite extraordinary for a regular person to catch even a glimpse of the ark's form, since it was covered with the shielding curtain, then a piece of durable leather, then a solid blue cloth. Since the ark of the covenant represented the presence of a holy God, it undoubtedly would have served as a call to holiness for everyone in the Israelite camp.

IT'S IMPORTANT TO GET A DEEP CLEANING NOW AND AGAIN, ESPECIALLY SINCE HOLINESS USHERS IN VICTORY.

In your present battle, you are being called to holiness as well. Don't try to hasten the purification process God is trying to do within you. It's important to get a deep cleaning now and again, especially since holiness ushers in victory.

5. GET THE SECRET INGREDIENT CALLED "ZEAL."

On a recent mission trip to the Dominican Republic, a preacher name Walt Wiley shared with our team the story of Nehemiah, a man who spearheaded rebuilding the walls of Jerusalem. I've read the book of Nehemiah many times, but Walt pointed out something I had never considered before. If you read through Nehemiah chapter 3, you will see how Nehemiah takes the time to list many of the people who worked with him on the Jerusalem wall project. Though it reads a bit like a telephone directory, you learn:

- WHO was building with Nehemiah—the names of the people and what they did in their regular, day-to-day careers (e.g., goldsmiths, perfume makers, and merchants);
- WHAT they were responsible for—the different aspects of building the Fish Gate, Fountain Gate, Tower of the Ovens, and the like;
- WHERE they worked—notice the references to "next to that" or "next section" throughout this passage of Scripture.

Walt said, "I read the chapter and learn who, what, and where, but only in one place does Nehemiah tell me *how* a person went about his job. In verse 20, one guy stood out to Nehemiah out of all the other people who were working. His name was Baruch, and the Bible says he 'zealously repaired' his section of the wall.

He went about his job with intense enthusiasm and devotion. Basically, Baruch whistled while he worked, praised God as he diligently laid one brick on top of another, and did it all with a smile on his face. Nehemiah must have thought, *Wow, this guy is truly exceptional!*"

Walt summed up this great lesson by asserting that the real test in your journey is not determined by who you are, what you're responsible for, or where you are. The real test is *how* you go about the little things in life, as well as the big things. "How" reveals your heart, and that is what matters to God.[9]

Just like the people in Nehemiah chapter 3, every one of us is building something. You might be building a family, a marriage, a relationship, a ministry, a company, a territory, or a church. You might be building your faith, strength, and courage as you strive to make walls fall down in your own personal Jericho. Whatever you are working at, you can make it a holy exercise by doing it zealously as Baruch did.

Whenever I talk to people who hate their jobs, I always attempt to encourage them by opening their eyes to the spiritual possibilities that paid positions provide. We all know that a job enables us to have money so we can afford a place to live and food to eat. But how many of us utilize the greater potential of using our homes to host a small-group Bible study in order to make a spiritual difference in the lives of others? When we take the money we've earned from our jobs and give God the first 10 percent—which is called a tithe (Mal. 3:6–12)—the church is then able to keep its doors open, pay its staff and utilities, dig wells in Africa, rescue and restore children and orphans, support missionaries who are taking the gospel into the four corners of the world, feed the hungry, provide medicine to the sick, and so much more.

Suddenly, this despised, humdrum job is tied to a significant spiritual assignment. It changes the way a person goes about his or her work and the attitude he or she has. It now brings a purpose to that job. Colossians 3:23–24 encourages us: "Whatever you do, work at it with all your heart, as working for the Lord, not for human masters, since you know that you will receive an inheritance from the Lord as a reward. It is the Lord Christ you are serving."

There aren't too many activities in life that could be as monotonous as pouring juice into tiny communion cups and filling trays with wafers. Many modern churches don't serve communion every weekend, they say, because they do not want the sacrament to become commonplace. But the more accurate reason, in my opinion, is because it takes too much time out of the worship service schedule. In the church I grew up in, we took communion every weekend, and we do the same at Shepherd Church today. At our main campus, we have about twenty-five volunteers who show up an hour before each of our five worship services begin every weekend to fill 9,200 communion cups with grape juice and dozens of trays with those itty-bitty pieces of bread.

My wife and I recently celebrated our twenty-fifth anniversary of pastoring at Shepherd. After all the fanfare, I thought about the volunteers at the church who hardly ever receive recognition or appreciation. I thought about the men and women who have been helping with communion every weekend, rain or shine, for the past twenty-five years. According to my calculations, they have probably filled at least *ten million* communion cups in that span of time.

I'm confident these faithful folks never considered this work to be dull or boring for two reasons. One, people don't give freely of their time unless they love what they're doing. Two, the task itself involves the symbolic body and blood of our Lord and Savior; it represents His great and wonderful sacrifice. It's my belief that the people who have been filling communion cups and trays for the past twenty-five years know they're taking part in a holy sacrament. With that understanding, a seemingly ordinary task becomes the best job in the world.

From the outside looking in, it may not have been very exciting to watch the priests in Joshua 6:6 go about the simple task of carrying the ark of the covenant around the walls of Jericho day after day for seven days. But they were engaged in a holy exercise, and I believe the priests were keenly aware of the great honor involved in their task.

Like the communion volunteers and the Israelite priests, you can see the holiness in any job or responsibility, no matter how big or small. When you do, suddenly you're not just taking your child to school; you're being a steward of a precious child who is going to do great things for God's kingdom. You're not just clocking in to work; you're bringing the light and love of Jesus to a place that desperately needs to see it. You're not just placing money in the offering plate; you're making an eternal impact. Your marriage is not just a union between a man and a woman; it's a spiritual picture—holy, divine, and sacred—of Christ and the church (Eph. 5:31–33).

In your quest to conquer your impossible obstacles, you might be doing the same thing every day, but you can take what seems ordinary and mundane and make it spiritual by praying, hoping, showing love and grace, and staying faithful. You can choose to do anything with zeal.

AN UNFORGETTABLE
PICTURE OF HOLINESS

If you had told me a couple of years ago that I would one day ride sixty to seventy miles on a road bicycle for fun, I'm not sure I would have believed you. But years of playing basketball and golf had finally caught up to me, causing major damage to the meniscal cartilage in my knee. I'd play a basketball game or a round of golf and literally not be able to walk afterward; that's how bad it had gotten. Knowing this, a friend recommended I try cycling as a way to stay in shape and maintain the competitiveness I love about sports, but with less strain on my knees. So I joined the cycling ministry at Shepherd Church, and I've been hooked ever since.

One day, as we were riding along the beach on the bike path in Santa Monica, I got to know Raul, one of the guys in our group. He started to tell me his testimony about how he got saved and how he came to church, and I almost fell off my bike. It's an incredible story I'd like to share with you.

Raul works on staff at Shepherd in our media arts department and always seems to serve with a smile on his face. He's covered with tattoos and doesn't resemble what I'd imagine a "church guy" looks like. I learned that Raul was born in Mexico. His mother and father were both alcoholics, and when Raul was three weeks old, his mother and father decided they didn't want to raise him. They brought their baby to the bar one night and got drunk. When they left the bar, they placed three-week-old Raul in a sack, left him on the sidewalk, and walked away.

His grandmother, the mother of his father, lived in California, but she happened to be in Mexico at the time. Being suspicious that something was up, she followed Raul's father and mother to the bar that night. When she saw that they had placed the baby in a sack and left him on the sidewalk, she took him and smuggled him back to California.

Raul's grandmother raised him until he was in the third grade. Then she sent him to live with her other son and paid him to raise the boy. Raul did not find out the man he thought was his father was actually his uncle—his biological father's brother—until he was forty years old. When he was in the sixth grade, Raul's uncle began abusing him. He never said a word to his grandmother because his uncle would threaten him, so he ran away from home and began living on the streets.

At night, he would climb up to the roof of the school and sleep near the warm vents that were just above the kitchen freezers. For food, he would wait on the docks of the local grocery store in the morning when they threw out old produce. He was in pure survival mode, afraid to ask anyone for help and cheating on tests to get through school. Eventually, his friends realized he was wearing the same clothes every day and that he was starting to smell. They made fun of him and distanced themselves from him. Soon he dropped out of school.

Raul said his life spiraled when his marriage to a high school girlfriend ended after just six months. He started partying and hanging out with a friend who was a drug addict. This friend later stole a vehicle, and Raul was accused of the crime even though he was on the other side of town. He spent sixty-six days in prison, but the description of the suspect did not match him; nor did the fingerprints police found on the van.

"When I went to court, the judge said, 'What kind of deal do you want?'" Raul explained. "I said, 'Give me probation.' I just wanted to get out of county jail; it was crazy in there."

Raul received probation and was released from jail. He moved to Minnesota and tried to start his life over. It didn't take long before Raul got involved with the wrong people and drugs all over again. He was arrested on May 14, 2004, and sent to Pine County Jail. Little did he know, his health was in jeopardy because of drug use, stress, lack of food, and not sleeping for two to three weeks at a time. On his first day in jail, he had a mild heart attack and was rushed to the hospital. His doctor told him he needed to stop doing drugs or else he would die.

When Raul went back to jail the next day, he found a letter on his bunk from his codefendant that read: "You need to be at an outreach meeting tomorrow at 6:30 p.m." Raul had no idea what that meant; he just thought he was going to get to talk to his codefendant and possibly get out of jail. So he went to the meeting, which was held in a small room packed with other guys like him. Raul didn't see his codefendant anywhere, so he turned to leave. But someone shut the door. He looked around and saw an empty chair near the front of the stuffy room. Raul walked through the crowd of men, sat in the empty chair, and put his head down. Suddenly, an old man named Jim walked into the room and started preaching, "Do you know God loves you so much He sent His only Son—" But Raul didn't want to hear any of it.

"At that point, I could care less about God," he said. "If there was a God, why would I have been abandoned as a baby and have all these terrible things happen to me? So I covered my ears with my hands and put my head between my knees. But the more Jim talked about God, the more I could hear him; I couldn't believe it. I was squeezing my head so hard I thought my eyes were going to pop out of their sockets!"

Raul said he was extremely angry when Jim finished talking. He decided he wasn't going to get up right away because he was so mad he knew he would probably hit somebody. So he looked to the left and to the right and saw people all around. He put his head back down, waited, and took a deep breath. He looked to the left and right again, and everyone was gone. Raul stood to his feet, but Jim, the old preacher man, was standing right in front of him.

He said to Raul, "Son, I see the Lord Jesus Christ working in your heart right now."

"I wanted to knock him out," Raul told me. "Why would he tell me something like that? So, I said, 'What?' And he put his finger over my heart and said, 'Son, I see the Lord Jesus Christ working in your heart right now.'"

Right at that moment, Raul said he believed. He heard a voice in his right ear that whispered, "Let there be light." He felt a pounding in his chest that went down to his legs and shock waves that went up his body and through his hands. Suddenly, he said, his arms were raised, he was asking for forgiveness, and he was crying like a baby.

"When a little child falls down and hurts himself," Raul shared, "he runs to his mother or father with his arms up because he knows they are going to pick him up. The child tries to catch his breath and talk, but he can't get the words out. That's how I was. It was the exact same thing. I was looking up with my arms raised, crying, and trying to catch my breath."

One of the deputies went toward Raul, but Jim said, "No, don't touch him. He's being filled by the Holy Ghost. Let him be; let him be. He's fine."

"I got arrested on the fourteenth of May and got saved on the sixteenth," Raul told me. "And I've been on fire for the Lord ever since!"

Raul served five and a half years in prison. There, he became involved in the Chuck Colson Ministry and learned about God's Word. His mentor encouraged him that God was using the time in prison to grow Raul and make him holy. The last literacy test he took in the prison system revealed he was reading at the level of a third grader, and people laughed at him. But he can read anything in the Bible. The Word of God is the only book he can read cover to cover with ease.

After Raul got out of prison, he moved back to California and his dentist invited him to Shepherd Church. He joined the church and started volunteering right away. Now we are blessed to have him as a full-time employee. I believe he will lead a church someday.

One of the miracles about the gospel is that you can't argue with the power of a changed life. I don't know anyone else besides Raul who was left in a paper sack as an infant and who reads at a third-grade level. Yet Raul serves the Lord with faithfulness and diligence. And you know what? He's one of the holiest men I know. This incredible testimony shows me that any wall can be conquered for God's glory.

> THIS CALL TO HOLINESS DOES NOT MEAN WE WON'T FACE STRUGGLES AND TEMPTATIONS; IT MEANS GOD'S GRACE GIVES US POWER TO OVERCOME.

No matter who you are or where you've been, you have an opportunity to become a new creation, a holy vessel for Jesus Christ. As 2 Timothy 1:9 puts it, "He has saved us and called us to a holy life—not because of anything we have done but because of his own purpose and grace." This call to holiness does not mean we won't face struggles and temptations; it means God's grace gives us power to overcome. No amount of physical strength, mental aptitude, cleverness, strategy, personality, or good looks is going to get you out of your current struggle. Only by placing God at the center of your walk, thereby making it a holy exercise, will you truly find victory.

Choosing to trust in God's holy plan rather than his own knowledge, Aryeh followed Joshua to the gathering of soldiers and priests. He stood by Joshua's side to show his full support and solidarity. First, Joshua called the priests and said to them, "Take up the ark of the covenant of the LORD and have seven priests carry trumpets in front of it." Then, he ordered the army, "Advance! March around the city, with an armed guard going ahead of the ark of the LORD."[10]

So the seven priests carrying seven trumpets went forward, blowing their trumpets, and the ark of the covenant followed them. The armed guard marched ahead of the priests who blew the trumpets, and the rear guard followed the ark. The Israelites marched around Jericho's wall once and returned to the camp, and they did this for six days. On the seventh day, they would march around the city seven times, in hopeful expectancy that the walls would come tumbling down.

A PRAYER FOR TODAY

Father, like the angels who surround Your throne in heaven, I cry out to You, "Holy, holy, holy is the Lord God Almighty!" You alone are worthy of this excellent exaltation. And yet, You command us to be holy because You are holy. So, will You please purify my heart and help me to be more like You? Your rightful place is at the center of everything I do, just as Your priests and the ark of the covenant were in the center of the procession that marched around Jericho. No matter what obstacles stand before me or the trials or temptations I face, give me the strength and wisdom to put You first in my life and approach every task with holiness, faithfulness, and zeal. I know that in doing so, I will obtain victory. In Jesus' name I pray, amen.

A CULTURE OF LIKE-MINDED PEOPLE

Surround yourself with other believers committed to the same goal.

In the still of the night, Eliakim quietly collected his belongings and stepped over his sleeping comrades. In the morning the priests and the armed men would make their fourth trek around the walls of Jericho. Eliakim wanted no part of it. He crept out of the camp, leaving behind his sword, which was cumbersome, and taking only a small dagger and the clothes on his back. He would have to find food on his journey. If he starved to death, so be it. Perhaps it was an appropriate fate for a defector.

A twig snapped beneath Eliakim's foot. Aryeh, the commander of the army, stirred and mumbled something unintelligible. Eliakim froze. If Aryeh caught him, he most certainly would be a dead man. The commander would pounce on him like a fierce lion and kill him in a heartbeat in order to make an example out of him to anyone who also might be considering treason. Eliakim was young, often teased by the other men for being so thin and short in stature, and he wouldn't stand a chance against Aryeh's strength and prowess.

Making sure the commander had settled back in to a deep slumber, Eliakim continued his stealthy escape. But as soon as he made it just outside of camp, he sensed he was being followed. As he gripped his dagger tightly, Eliakim tried to figure out his next move. What he was lacking in size he more than made up for in cleverness. In a flash, he turned to the right and ducked into a sparse patch of desert shrubs. Crouching low as he ran, Eliakim could hear the footsteps behind him still in pursuit. But the brush could only cover him for a short distance before it cleared and revealed the open desert once again.

"Where are you going, Eliakim?" a voice called to him. There seemed to be an air of concern in the voice rather than anger, but it was probably a trick. Eliakim bolted as fast as his legs could go. His pursuer caught up with him quickly and tackled him to the ground. It was dark, so Eliakim could not see the face of the man who was about to take his life, but clearly the man was bigger and stronger than the young deserter. He wrestled the dagger away from Eliakim with little effort, and the young man's struggle to get away was futile.

Though he was nearly out of breath, Eliakim managed to shout, "Who are you?"

"Don't be afraid, Eliakim," the man said. "It is I, Joshua. I'm going to let you go now, but do not run away. I want to talk to you."

Eliakim's heart pounded and his mind raced. Could this be true—he had been found by Joshua, the leader of the Israelites?

A brave and mighty man, Joshua fought and overcame the Amalekites under the direction of Moses. Then, the authority God had given Moses transferred to Joshua when Moses died. Eliakim feared that with one word from Joshua, fire from heaven could rain down and smite him. Surely this was worse a fate than being discovered by Aryeh or starving in the wilderness!

Joshua released Eliakim from his grip and stood to his feet, helping the young man up as well. "Eliakim, why are you fleeing, and where were you going?"

"I don't know," Eliakim replied, looking at the ground. He was too ashamed to look at Joshua's face. "Maybe I'll return to Egypt and work as a slave, or join some traveling merchants or herders."

"Why?" Joshua asked.

"Because I'm not cut out for all of this—marching around the wall, storming some impossibly shut-up city, and taking possession of it."

"Why do you feel you're not cut out for this mission? You might not be the tallest of my soldiers, but you are shrewd and your spirit is strong."

"Right," Eliakim said sarcastically. "Do what you must to me, Joshua, here in the desert. I'm ready. Only do not take me back to the camp to suffer my demise in front of the rest of our people."

"Eliakim," Joshua said with compassion, "I'm not going to harm you."

"You're not?" The young man looked up at Joshua to see if he could detect any duplicity in his leader's eyes.

"No," Joshua replied. "I just want to understand why you would leave when we are so close to victory."

"Because I'm *afraid*!" cried Eliakim. "This plan of marching around the walls makes no sense to me, and I'm afraid we won't be successful. I'm afraid I'll be captured by one of those uncircumcised Jerichoites and be murdered. I'm afraid I will never have a family and that I'll never amount to anything besides being 'little Eliakim' who should never have become a soldier in the first place!"

Eliakim collapsed onto the ground and began to weep. Joshua crouched down next to him and collected his thoughts. He remembered well how the fire of the Lord burned among those who complained about their hardships in the desert and how His anger was aroused against those who rejected Him and regretted leaving Egypt.[1] Joshua recalled how the people later rebelled at Kadesh in the Desert of Paran, and how God swore that none of the grumblers would see the promised land.[2] But Joshua recognized that Eliakim was not someone who simply wanted to complain. This was a young man who was afraid. Joshua was moved with compassion.

"Eliakim, listen to me," Joshua said. "There's no reason to be afraid. The Lord is with us. He said to me, 'See, I have delivered Jericho into your hands, along with its king and its fighting men.'[3] He promised, and the victory is ours for the taking! Don't you see?"

The young man continued to look down at the ground as tears dripped down the bridge of his nose and made a small pool in the dirt reflecting the moonlight between his feet. Joshua stood once again and helped Eliakim to his feet. He handed the young soldier his dagger and placed his cloak, which had been lying on the ground after their tussle, back upon his shoulders. Eliakim looked bewildered.

"No matter how much the other men might tease you and poke fun, they are your brothers," Joshua told him. "Joking around and giving each other a hard time is what soldiers do, but we always stand with one another when it comes to our mission."

Eliakim wiped his tears with the back of his hand.

"The choice is yours," Joshua told him. "You can come back and join your comrades, for we will surely take possession of this land the Lord has promised to us. Or you can continue on your way, and you might make it back to Egypt alone or join with the Canaanites who live in the hill country. But they are not your people."

Then the Israelite leader turned and returned to the camp.

⁓

Day 4 represents the halfway mark in our quest to see the walls fall down. But like Eliakim, there are people who give up when they're on the verge of victory. One of the main reasons this happens among believers is that they've attempted to fight a difficult battle alone or to embark upon the Christian walk without the support and accountability of other men and women of faith. Inevitably, the person grows weary of trying to persevere until victory is obtained.

But in any struggle we may face, we absolutely and unequivocally need to surround ourselves with like-minded individuals who can uplift our spirits, remind us of the truth, and cheer us on in achieving our goals. As you seek to bring down the walls in your personal Jericho, it's paramount that you garner strength and encouragement from other believers—especially the ones who have

> AS YOU SEEK TO BRING DOWN THE WALLS IN YOUR PERSONAL JERICHO, IT'S PARAMOUNT THAT YOU GARNER STRENGTH AND ENCOURAGEMENT FROM OTHER BELIEVERS— ESPECIALLY THE ONES WHO HAVE BEEN THROUGH WHAT YOU'RE GOING THROUGH AND CAN SHOW YOU THE WAY.

been through what you're going through and can show you the way.

Imagine being dropped off at the edge of a large forest or a vast desert plain. You are given a map that clearly shows you a straight path that would lead you to the other side of the forest or desert in no time at all. My guess is that the most difficult section would be the halfway mark. Perhaps you look around and all you see are thick trees or miles of sand with only an occasional cactus here and there.

You might begin to doubt that you're going to get through that stretch of land. You're alone. Your mouth gets dry, and your stomach begins to rumble. You've been walking for hours, and it doesn't appear that you're really making any progress. If you turn around, you might get lost or die of thirst or starvation. If you give up, you would face a similar fate.

Now imagine having expert travelers accompanying you on this mission. They can't do the work for you, but they can be by your side, encouraging you and giving you wise counsel. "We'll walk with you," they would say, "and together we will help each other get through this difficult ordeal." They would tell you that in the time it would take you to walk back to your starting point, you could be at the finish line. They would advise that the best thing to do is to stay the course, having faith that you're going to make it to your destination.

Whenever we try to get through a difficult season or a daunting problem, it's common to feel alone and afraid, and it's tempting to want to throw in the towel and walk away. Oftentimes we assume we're the only person going through this unique set of circumstances. In doing so, we fail to realize there are millions who have walked down this same road, stayed the course, and experienced complete and total triumph.

You will learn one powerful truth in this fourth chapter of our journey: there is immeasurable value in gathering support from other believers who are walking or have walked in your set of circumstances. This is being in a culture of like-minded people. In Joshua 6, God selected men who were united in mind-set and mission to march around the walls of Jericho. Their unity was a key factor that led to the city's ultimate defeat, and this shows us that having support from other believers is an indispensable step toward success.

WHAT DO YOU HAVE IN MIND?

Besides a few priests, the men who walked around the Jericho fortress were soldiers, men who were prepared to fight shoulder to shoulder and sword to sword. If you've ever observed men and women in the military in the midst of foot drills, you know that everyone is clothed in the same crisp uniform with the same stoic expression on his or her face. Like geese flying in *V* formation, these soldiers march in perfect harmony as one controlled unit. They all have the same mind-set and the same mission. Likewise as believers, in order for you and I to obtain victory in all areas of life, we must be unified and adopt the same mind-set, which is the mind of Christ.

What is the mind of Christ? We learn from the Scriptures that Jesus' mind was set upon doing the will of His Father in heaven and submitting to Him, even to the point of death on a cross.[4] During His life on earth, we see that Jesus had the mind-set of truth, love, and compassion because He:

- healed the sick (Matt. 19:2)
- fed the hungry (Matt. 15:29–39)
- forgave sinners (Matt. 9:6)
- showed grace (John 1:16)
- served others (Mark 10:45)
- prayed for the believers and the world (John 17)
- spent time with the cast-offs (Luke 5:30–31)
- preached with power (Matt. 5–7)

Jesus' motivation was His love for God and His love for all mankind, and our passion will be the same if we strive to be like Christ. Moreover, it's only logical that we will unite with other believers who desire to do the same.

People naturally converge with others who are passionate about the same things they are. Whenever I go to a Dodgers base-ball game in Los Angeles where I live, almost the entire stadium is filled with men, women, and children proudly sporting their Dodger blue. But I'm a St. Louis Cardinals fan, and we wear red. Anytime I see other folks walking around the stadium wearing a crimson Cardinals T-shirt, jersey, hat, or other gear, we'll give each other a high five and talk about how we hope to beat the Dodgers today. We're perfect strangers but we already share the common bond of supporting the Redbirds.

As believers, our number-one passion should not be our favorite sports teams, our occupations, our political affiliations, or even our roles as a spouse or a parent. We ought to be captivated by our love for an awesome God who gave His best for us, and our desire should be to give our best to Him. It's waking up every morning and setting our minds upon what we can do that would demonstrate our love for the Lord and our desire to do His will. It's that simple.

> JESUS' MOTIVATION WAS HIS LOVE FOR GOD AND HIS LOVE FOR ALL MANKIND, AND OUR PASSION WILL BE THE SAME IF WE STRIVE TO BE LIKE CHRIST.

Joshua and the Israelites did the will of God by being united together and following His clear instructions for Jericho's defeat. As noted earlier, all who were involved in the mission were either priests or soldiers. They were of the same profession, faith, and culture—united in the same task with the same mind-set and goal. As Christians, you and I most likely have different professions and come from different cultures. We may not look the same or have the same backgrounds or experiences, but we have the same faith, and we can adopt the same mind-set.

Having the mind-set of Christ can have a powerful influence on those around you. I remember hearing a story once about a high school that was having a homecoming dance. Every year, someone would throw a huge party afterward where there would be underage drinking. At a school assembly one day, a Christian girl stood up and announced that she and her parents were going to open up their home for an alcohol-free party as an alternative. As this young lady and her family made their preparations for the party, they were unsure whether or not anyone would come, but hundreds of students showed up at their home that night. All it took was one person who had a Christlike mind-set and offered a positive substitute for the cultural norm, and others joined in.

On the flip side, a worldly mind-set is also quite infectious. If you're going through a difficult time and you seek the counsel of people who don't know the Lord, the advice they're going to give you will be very different from the advice a Christian would give you. If you're married and you're hanging out with miserable couples that tear each other down and talk about divorce, it won't be long before you adopt that type of negative thinking. If you spend time with friends who get drunk, hang out at the bar or the nightclubs, smoke, curse, or gossip, you'll begin to do the same. It's almost impossible not to, for the Bible says, "Do not be misled: 'Bad company corrupts good character'" (1 Cor. 15:33).

Now don't get me wrong; this does not mean in any way that you should isolate yourself from unbelievers. First Corinthians 5:9–10 affirms that trying to do so would be impossible. Besides, Jesus Himself was compelled to reach out to the *unreached* and the unloved—those whom the religious considered a lost cause. He engaged with them, spoke the truth, and showed them love. But Christ's core group of people—the men and women He spent the most time with—were committed followers who yearned to know God. As believers in our Lord and Savior, our minds should be set on the same mission.

Now that we understand what it means to adopt the mind of Christ, let's explore five reasons why being in a culture of like-minded believers is an important key to spiritual victory.

1. IN BATTLE THERE IS STRENGTH IN NUMBERS.

Whenever you're engaged in battle of any kind, there is always strength in numbers. It's interesting to note that on more than one occasion in the Old Testament, God required Israel to count the number of soldiers they had. In Numbers 1:2–3, God told Moses:

> Take a census of the whole Israelite community by their clans and families, listing every man by name, one by one. You and Aaron are to count according to their divisions all the men in Israel who are twenty years old or more and able to serve in the army.

Later, in Numbers 26:1–4, as Israel prepared to enter the promised land, God commanded a second census to be taken not only to evaluate the military, but also to prepare for future property allocation in Canaan. He said, "From the whole community of Israel, record the names of all the warriors by their families. List all the men twenty years old or older who are able to go to war" (NLT). When the leaders counted the fighting men within all the tribes of Israel, the number totaled 601,730 (v. 51). That's a big army!

Similarly, the church of Jesus Christ is a big family. It's estimated that there are more than two billion Christians worldwide, which is almost one-third of the entire world's population.[5] You and I are literally surrounded by other believers, and there is strength whenever we're united together—especially when we are facing obstacles in our personal lives.

But as a sheep that wanders away from the safety of the

shepherd and the rest of the flock, when a Christian attempts to go through the challenges of life alone, he or she is easy pickings for the devil. He wants nothing more than for you to become steeped in the world and return to your former way of life so that you don't fulfill the greater purpose God has for you.

> THE DEVIL WANTS NOTHING MORE THAN FOR YOU TO BECOME STEEPED IN THE WORLD AND RETURN TO YOUR FORMER WAY OF LIFE SO THAT YOU DON'T FULFILL THE GREATER PURPOSE GOD HAS FOR YOU.

Look at what 1 Peter 5:8 says: "Be alert and of sober mind. Your enemy the devil prowls around like a roaring lion looking for someone to devour." He will use any and every excuse to draw you away from the church for your ultimate destruction. That might sound extreme, but Jesus Himself said in John 10:10 that our enemy has but three goals: to steal, kill, and destroy.

I've seen it happen a thousand times. Men and women stop going to church because something has offended them or they don't make time for worship in their busy schedules. They get away from accountability, from like-minded people in the faith. Not long after, it is heartbreaking to observe how far they have fallen away.

What if one of the Israelite soldiers had decided to abandon his place in line at the wall of Jericho and head back to camp? He would say to his comrades, "Hey, you know what? I'm going to go back to my tent and fix myself a sandwich and maybe count the goats." That soldier would have missed out on the miracle that was getting ready to happen. It would have been his great loss. (And had enough soldiers left their posts, there wouldn't have been an army—let alone a victory—to speak of today.) Similarly, whenever we choose to go out on our own and stop gathering together with other believers in the Lord's house, we miss out on experiencing Him in a personal way and seeing the miracles He is doing in and through the church.

Don't allow the devil's schemes to lure you away from the church and to steal, kill, and destroy the joy of being a part of God's plan and rewarding relationships with fellow believers. If someone in the church has offended you, pray for him or her and forgive him or her. If you don't feel that a particular ministry is being effective, go to the leader with a humble heart and ask how you can help. If you have done all that sincerely and you still don't feel that the church you're attending is right for you, then visit another church and give it an earnest effort until you find a church where you feel at home.

Since there isn't a perfect church in the world, just as there isn't a perfect Christian in the world, we have to show one another grace.

> And let us consider how we may spur one another on toward love and good deeds, not giving up meeting together, as some are in the habit of doing, but encouraging one another—and all the more as you see the Day approaching. (Heb. 10:24–25)

In John 17, Jesus looked up toward heaven and prayed for Himself and for His disciples. Afterward, He prayed for believers "that all of them may be one, Father, just as you are in me and I am in you. May they also be in us *so that the world may believe that you have sent me*" (v. 21, emphasis added). This means that when believers are bonded together in love, unity, and like-mindedness, people who don't believe in the gospel will look at us and understand that God sent Jesus Christ into the world. That is a very powerful cause and effect. If taken seriously by Christians, it would lead the entire world to salvation. Being in a culture of like-minded people not only benefits us in our personal battles, but it also benefits in the bigger picture of God's plan. He wants the world to come to know Christ (John 3:16; 2 Peter 3:9).

Unity is such a powerful force that it can sometimes result in unfavorable consequences as well. It reminds me of the story of the Tower of Babel in Genesis 11, which occurred during a time when the whole world had a common language. The descendants of Noah disobeyed God's command in Genesis 9:1 to fill the entire earth; instead they banded together and traveled eastward (Gen. 11:2).[6] One day, they decided to build a great tower that would reach the heavens. The Lord saw this and said, "If as one people speaking the same language they have begun to do this, then nothing they plan to do will be impossible for them. Come, let us go down and confuse their language so they will not understand each other" (Gen. 11:6–7). So God scattered the people and confused their language, and the people stopped building the great Tower of Babel.

People who are of one heart, mind, and accord are a force to be reckoned with. When believers are united, our witness increases in effectiveness and others take notice. In Acts 2:42–47, we see how the Holy Spirit was unleashed upon believers like a rushing wind and emboldened them to preach the gospel with passion. Those who accepted the good news devoted themselves to preaching the Word and to prayer. Verse 44 tells us, "All the believers were together and had everything in common." They sold their possessions and gave to anyone as he or she had need. They ate together in one another's homes with sincere and happy hearts, and they praised God. Then we see the ultimate result of their unity in verse 47: "And the Lord added to their number daily those who were being saved."

The extraordinary harmony exhibited by the early church caught the attention of unbelievers. As a result, thousands of people accepted the gospel. And you know what? It's 100 percent possible for contemporary Christians to be as unified and effective as these early believers. We simply need to remember we have strength in our numbers and come together in love, passion, and commitment.

2. THERE IS REAL VALUE WHEN SOLDIERS ARE COMMITTED TO A COMMON GOAL.

While there is undeniable strength in numbers, it's quite possible that the real value comes from soldiers working side by side, committed to a common goal. Just as the Israelite soldiers and priests were united together in purpose—their minds set on the same task and the same mission—we need dedicated people in our corner if we want to be successful at causing the walls to fall down in our lives. It doesn't matter if this group of people is large or small. The key is commitment. Allow me to share with you an example of this point in Scripture.

Are you familiar with the unusual story of Gideon and the three hundred men who defeated the Midianites in Judges 7? I'll give you a quick summary. The Bible says that the sins of Israel became so great that God allowed the Midianites to oppress the Israelites severely for seven years. The Midianites ravaged the land, destroying the Israelites' livestock and crops. God's people were so destitute that they finally cried out to Him for help.

So the Lord called an unassuming young man named Gideon to save Israel. At first, Gideon organized an army of tens of thousands of soldiers who prepared to attack the Midianites, but God said to him:

"You have too many men. I cannot deliver Midian into their hands, or Israel would boast against me, 'My own strength has saved me.' Now announce to the army, 'Anyone who trembles with fear may turn back and leave Mount Gilead.'" So twenty-two thousand men left, while ten thousand remained. (Judges 7:2–3)

But there were still too many men, so God told Gideon to take his army down to the Spring of Harod and He would thin them out there. The Lord told Gideon that the men who drank water from cupped hands, lapping like dogs, would be the ones who would defeat the Midianites; the men who knelt down to drink should be sent home.

This might sound like a silly way to choose an army, but consider how a soldier must always be alert. If he stops to drink water from a stream or a lake, he can still be on the lookout if he remains upright and brings the water to his mouth with cupped hands. But the soldier who kneels down to the water not only puts himself in a vulnerable position, but also limits his ability to watch out for danger. In the story of Gideon, only three hundred men brought the water up to their mouths with cupped hands and lapped it up like dogs, and that's the group that the Lord used to conquer the Midianites (vv. 22–25).

Truth be told, I'd rather have three hundred committed men who were always prepared and looking out for the entire group than a thousand men who were only looking out for themselves. In your walk with Christ, these are the people—no matter how few—who speak the truth in love and support your vision. They encourage you to keep fighting and pressing on until you are triumphant.

When I first joined the cycling ministry at Shepherd, we would occasionally come across a particular twenty-foot-high hill that I just couldn't get up. It was painful, and it seemed impossible. But you know what? After six months of working hard and building up my strength and endurance, I was able to conquer not only that twenty-foot hill, but also something far greater when I decided to join my buddies in tackling Mount Baldy, which is more than ten thousand feet of elevation to climb—one pedal at a time.[7]

At the seventeen-mile mark, we stopped. I pretended it was because I wanted to take a group photo, but really it was because I was certain I was dying. I needed to rest. When we finally made it all the way to the top, I felt a huge sense of accomplishment. A few days later, my friend Raul, whose testimony I shared in day 3, e-mailed me a photo of a grizzly bear riding a tricycle. He wrote, "This bear saw you and he wanted to try it." That made me laugh. Hard. But a serious lesson I learned from the whole experience is that it doesn't matter whether it's a big hill or a little hill—it's always challenging and it's always painful. However, the climb is easier to endure when you have like-minded individuals accompanying you in your journey.

When the road-cycling team and I get together and ride, we call it a "Party of Pain." It's all about managing how much pain you can tolerate. As I struggled to ascend that formidable mountain, the small group of cyclers who accompanied me couldn't do the hard work for me, but they encouraged me when the climb seemed impossible. These men were committed to the same task and the same goal I was, and it made all the difference.

You may only know two or three people right now who are sincere, committed Christians. It would be more beneficial for you to link up with those two or three people than a dozen worldly friends who have no concept of eternal matters and don't care a lick about your spiritual health and growth. You have a choice, just as Joshua 24:15 declares so powerfully:

> But if serving the LORD seems undesirable to you, then choose for yourselves this day whom you will serve, whether the gods your ancestors served beyond the Euphrates, or the gods of the Amorites, in whose land you are living. But as for me and my household, we will serve the LORD.

If everyone around you is serving the god of money or the god of fashion, alcohol, drugs, sex, or ambition, or the god of self, find that small group of people who are serving the real God and hang with those people. Why go along with the crowd? Choose to be in a culture of people who are committed to matters of eternal importance.

> CHOOSE TO BE IN A CULTURE OF PEOPLE WHO ARE COMMITTED TO MATTERS OF ETERNAL IMPORTANCE.

When Jesus traveled and healed people in Galilee, Jerusalem, Judea, and the regions across the Jordan, large crowds followed Him. But once He began saying strange things like "Whoever eats my flesh and drinks my blood remains in me, and I in them," the Bible says that many of His followers deserted Him (John 6:56–66). Then Jesus turned to the twelve disciples and asked them if they wanted to leave as well.

Peter replied, "Lord, to whom shall we go? You have the words of eternal life" (v. 68). Masses of people hung out with Jesus when He was performing great miracles such as healing afflictions, turning water into wine, and feeding thousands. But only a few people stood at the foot of the cross during His darkest hour.

In your current struggle, your true friends are the few people who will stick with you whether you're in the trenches or on top of the world. And your most reliable and trustworthy friend—Jesus— said He would be with you every step of the way (Heb. 13:5). Always remember that though a huge army of supporters may not always surround you, there is enormous value in being flanked by two or three or four followers of Christ who are committed to the same mission you are.

3. SUCCESS OFTEN REQUIRES THE HELP OF VETERANS.

As I write, it's Shark Week on the Discovery Channel. If you're brave enough to watch this weeklong series dedicated solely to sharks, you'll learn about many different species of this fierce predator, see some pretty cool (albeit frightening) underwater footage, and hear tale after tale of people getting attacked by sharks—all while being assured that sharks don't mean to harm humans. Ha! It never fails that some segment will show a man or a woman in an underwater cage getting up close and personal with great whites, bull sharks, tiger sharks, or hammerheads. Did you know you could do the same thing in Hawaii or Australia or most other tropical vacation spots? It's called "swimming with sharks." Now, on the off chance I suddenly had a lapse in sanity and decided to go and swim with sharks, I would want to go with the experts—the people who have done it many times and know what they're doing. Wouldn't you?

In the battle you're facing today, you're swimming with the sharks just by being a Christian in modern culture. We live in a world in which just about everyone is looking out for themselves and pursuing worldly gain. When you seek to live a righteous life according to the Word of God, it's as if you're swimming in an ocean full of sharks with a tiny cut on your toe—people of the world are sure to smell blood and zero in on you. That's because your integrity and godliness invite attacks from people of the world who don't possess the mind of Christ.

But you will survive and obtain true victory of eternal worth if you travel with veterans. In your battle, seek out like-minded and mature people in the faith who have been where you are today and can give you the spiritual tools necessary to equip you on your journey. They know how to navigate through shark-invested waters and come out stronger, and they can teach you how to do the same in your current struggle.

In his book, *Walking with God on the Road You Never Wanted to Travel*, Mark Atteberry discussed this same concept. He wrote:

> It would be ideal if your traveling companion happened to be an older, more experienced Christian, though it certainly wouldn't be a prerequisite. It's just that wiser and more experienced Christians tend to naturally pull us up toward their level, which is important when your spirits are sagging to begin with.[8]

Think about it. Whether you're swimming with sharks, hiking through a dense wilderness, rock climbing, or doing any activity that carries an element of danger or uncertainty, you are potentially putting your life at risk simply by embarking on the adventure in the first place. You need to be accompanied by someone who knows what he or she is doing. And if we're talking about battle—like the one Joshua and the Israelites were facing at Jericho—the stakes are even higher.

If I were placed in the middle of a battlefield, I'd want to be next to a veteran—the person who has combat experience and knows what kind of peril to look for, how to use his or her weapon, and how to survive harsh environments on limited food and water. I have so much admiration and appreciation for those who serve or have served in the military. These men and women have put their lives at risk and sacrificed greatly in order to protect our freedom. I'd want to be flanked by one of these seasoned soldiers who could show me the ropes and look out for me. That's where I'd be the safest. That's where I'd have the best chance of experiencing victory on the battlefield and seeing my walls fall down.

4. YOUR ENEMY WILL EMPLOY MANY TACTICS TO DEFEAT YOU.

The fourth reason that being in a culture of like-minded people is a significant step to spiritual victory is that the devil, your enemy, seeks to defeat you by utilizing several different tactics.

DISTRACTION

First, he will attempt to distract you from what's important. All week long we are busy and distracted by our careers, the television, the Internet, and the little arguments here and there. One day, we wake up and find that we're not even in the battle anymore—that we've gotten off the path entirely. But being together in church centers and refocuses us. Gathered with the body of believers to worship God and hear the Word of God, we remember, "Oh, *that's* the voice I should be listening to. *That's* what I should be doing. *That's* what's really important."

In Joshua 6, the priests and armed men all possessed a singular focus as they marched around the walls of Jericho, and they would not be distracted from their objective. They held fast to God's warning in Deuteronomy 18:9: "When you enter the land the LORD your God is giving you, do not learn to imitate the detestable ways of the nations there." So instead of abandoning their post to go party with the locals, they did exactly as God commanded them.

When I think about how this small group of men followed the commands of the Lord while everyone else in the region did his or her own thing and followed false gods, it reminds me of the narrow gate and the wide road that Jesus described in Matthew 7:13–14. "Enter through the narrow gate," He said. "For wide is the gate and broad is the road that leads to destruction, and many enter through it. But small is the gate and narrow the road that leads to life, and only a few find it."

Imagine a huge, multilane freeway with hundreds of cars speeding southbound. If you live in a big, crowded city as I do, this image is not difficult to visualize; it's your everyday reality. Now imagine if city officials decided to put a skinny bike lane smack-dab in the middle of that busy highway—going northbound. You're either on the busy freeway in your safe car with all the other people who are driving south, or you're on your bicycle in a tiny lane in the middle of that freeway, pedaling as fast as you can and heading north. What if someone gave you the inside scoop that all those lanes going south were headed straight for the city dump, but the slender bike lane took its travelers straight to a gorgeous beach, a veritable paradise just outside the city? Which lane would you choose?

I'd choose the bike lane, without question—and that's not just because I'm an avid cyclist. Sure, this path looks difficult. It might seem as though there aren't many other cyclists in that lane with you. You may feel as though you're a little fish swimming upstream. But the wide road—the easy one that everyone else is traveling down—leads to spiritual death. And the skinny road—the one that takes discipline, courage, and effort, the one in which few people are traveling—leads to victory and eternal life.

DISCOURAGEMENT

Next, the enemy will try to discourage you with your circumstances. I won't spend too much time on this topic since the essence of this idea was covered in day 1, which examined the greatness of God in relation to the size of our problems. But put yourself in the shoes of a soldier in battle for a moment. These men and women are away from their loved ones, engaged in combat, and witnessing terribly traumatic events day in and day out. A recent study found that for every one hundred Iraq and Afghanistan war veterans, eleven to twenty of them will suffer from post-traumatic stress disorder.[9]

To be involved in a battle, whether physical or spiritual, for an extended period of time can be extremely discouraging, and the devil knows this. If he can depress you through your circumstances, he will attempt to defeat you in every way possible. But it will be very difficult for him to accomplish this if you are surrounded by other believers who will encourage you to stay focused on the power of God rather than the disheartening aspects of your current circumstances.

SIN

When all else fails, your enemy will attempt to destroy you with sin. We are God's people living in a fallen world, and there

are many temptations to lure us away from the faith. The believers
in the ancient city of Ephesus faced these same temptations. Paul
urged them not to live as the rest of the world did. He said this
kind of thinking—characterized by sensuality, indulgence in every
kind of impurity, and greed—is futile and ignorant. He wrote in
Ephesians 4:20–24:

> That, however, is not the way of life you learned when you
> heard about Christ and were taught in him in accordance with
> the truth that is in Jesus. You were taught, with regard to your
> former way of life, to put off your old self, which is being cor-
> rupted by its deceitful desires; to be made new in the attitude of
> your minds; and to put on the new self, created to be like God
> in true righteousness and holiness.

Paul went on to encourage the Ephesians to speak truthfully to
one another, not to allow anger to cause them to sin, not to steal,
to be productive, to share with those in need, to show compassion,
and to forgive. He warned them not to give the devil the slightest
open door in which to enter their lives and not to grieve the Holy
Spirit by engaging in sin (Eph. 4:25–32). Just like the Ephesians,
you and I must put away our old sinful desires, knowing that sin is
our enemy's favorite tool to destroy us in battle.

5. RIDICULE IS INEVITABLE.

Just as committed believers will help you guard against the enemy's
tactics, they also will help protect against the sting of mockery and
insults the world may hurl at you because you've chosen God's way.
This is the final reason being in a culture of like-minded people is
an important key to your ultimate victory. During your battle, it's

inevitable that you will face ridicule from others, and you need the support of believers to help you stay focused.

People of the world do not understand when they observe faithful Christians marching to the beat of God's drum, which is His way and His Word. In the case of Joshua and the Battle of Jericho, God basically said to His people, "I'm asking you to walk around the walls, and if you do what I'm asking you to do, you will have victory." The Israelites obeyed, and the first few days of their mission were probably peaceful and relatively uneventful. But as I touched upon briefly in day 2, it's possible that the Jerichoites' initial fear of the Israelites turned into mockery when they saw that these would-be invaders had been walking around their city for days without any obvious results.

Not one pebble had moved besides the dust the Israelite priests and armed men kicked around with their sandals while they marched. Perhaps jeering and insults could be heard in the native tongue of their enemies who stood at the top of the wall.

"*These* are the men we were so afraid of, just a few days ago?" one of them may have questioned.

"All they are doing is walking in circles," another might have yelled. "What fools!"

But I imagine Joshua saying to his fellow soldiers, "Don't answer their taunts. Don't say a word. Keep your mouths shut and stick with the plan."

God's people have always been mocked when they obey His commands. Can you imagine how Noah must have looked as he built that great big ark in the middle of the desert with no sign of rain (Gen. 6:11–22)? What a spectacle! His neighbors probably wandered over from time to time, and said, "Hey, Noah! What are you doing? Are you out of your mind?" Stifling laughter, they may have said, "Hey, Noah, it must stink in there with all those animals. You've got to be dumber than one of those donkeys you have up there in your ark. When is this so-called flood supposed to come anyway?"

Or imagine how Jesus must have looked as He hung upon the cross. Roman soldiers fashioned a crown of thorns, placed it upon Jesus' head, and mocked Him by calling Him "the King of the Jews." From the ground below, people shouted, "He saved others, but he can't save himself! He's the king of Israel! Let him come down now from the cross, and we will believe in him!" (Matt. 27:42).

The apostle Paul was beaten, shipwrecked, imprisoned, and without food or clothing at times. As he and other Christians were persecuted because of their faith, Paul wrote, "For it seems to me that God has put us apostles on display at the end of the procession, like those condemned to die in the arena. We have been made a spectacle to the whole universe, to angels as well as to human beings" (1 Cor. 4:9).

Worldwide, more Christians were martyred in the twentieth century than in all previous centuries combined.[10] We don't think much of Christian persecution in America and other developed nations, but the tide is turning. As we discussed earlier, no matter where you turn—whether it's the media, politics, or public opinion—biblical values are ridiculed and rejected. Believers are scorned for revering and obeying God's Word.

The high school or college student who strives to remain pure until his or her wedding day is often met with teasing and pressure to conform to the idea that premarital sex is "no big deal." The faithful husband or wife is constantly bombarded by messages from peers and the media that he or she ought to be loyal to his or her desires and not to his or her spouse. The person who refuses to fudge a little on his or her taxes is called foolish by "financially savvy" individuals.

The reality is that we live in a world where good is called evil and evil is called good (Isa. 5:20). And if Shakespeare was correct when he wrote, "All the world's a stage," then the people of this world are sitting in the audience, watching us Christians with our strange beliefs and our commitment to walk with God by faith. They point their fingers and laugh at us because the manner in which we live is so foreign to them that it's amusing. The Bible actually says we are foreigners in this world (1 Peter 2:11), and Jesus Himself said that though we are in the world, we are not of the world (John 17:15–16).

This world is not our home, and we are strangers in a culture that does not understand spiritual matters because worldly people lack the Holy Spirit. First Corinthians 2:14 tells us that, "The person without the Spirit does not accept the things that come from the Spirit of God but considers them foolishness, and cannot understand them because they are discerned only through the Spirit." People of the world can't comprehend why we believers act and speak the way we do. So doesn't it make sense that we ought to band together with other Christians who are able to perceive the same spiritual truths and are committed to the same goal?

As I've said before, this doesn't mean we shouldn't befriend those who don't know Christ, in hopes of showing them God's love and truth. But many believers make the mistake of blending in and fitting in with the world. I call this kind of person an undercover Christian. No one really knows that he or she believes in Jesus because he or she never shares it verbally or ever shows it. Instead, this person uses the same coarse language, dresses the same way, watches the same television shows and movies, listens to the same music, and engages in the same activities as worldly people.

This should not be. As believers, you and I are engaged in a spiritual battle where the line has been clearly drawn in the sand. Just as Joshua and the Israelites knew they were God's people and were fighting His battle, we as Christians need to remember who we belong to and what our mission is. We are God's people, and we are called to stand for His Word.

When the world mocks you because of your Christian values, it will be much easier for you to stand for what you believe if you are immersed in a culture of like-minded followers of Jesus. United as one, Joshua and the Israelites easily would have endured any derision that may have come from the Jerichoites as they marched around the walls. Likewise, you ought to unite together with other like-minded believers in order to find strength in battle and withstand worldly opposition. In doing so, you will be one step closer to victory.

WE ARE THE CHAMPIONS

The church of Jesus Christ is the largest family in the world. You could go to any nation across the seven seas and find people who love the Lord and desire to serve Him wholeheartedly. Any like-minded individual could walk into a Christian church anywhere in the world and be welcomed into that body of believers. Whether in the mission field in Africa, the underground church in China, or the contemporary church in Australia, you instantly will find spiritual mothers, fathers, brothers, and sisters when you adopt the mind and heart of Christ.

You and I are not alone on this journey. We are part of a body of believers that has been called to participate in and fulfill God's purposes. Our mission is the same, though we each may have a different role to play. Athletes who are fully committed to their team operate with the understanding that they're not alone on the team, and that it takes working together with other members of the team intentionally and harmoniously to ensure victory.

Pat Riley, who was named NBA Coach of the Year three times and won numerous championships, has a theory called "the Disease of Me." Whenever a team would win an NBA championship, he noticed that winning it the following year seemed more difficult than the first time. That's because each player had sacrificed something for the common good when they won the first championship. But afterward, players started focusing on themselves. They wanted to get paid more, take more shots, get more playing time, or get more endorsement deals. They would feel frustrated, underappreciated, and resentful—even when the team performed successfully. Selfishly, they would attempt to outshine other members of the team.[11]

Without a doubt, focusing on oneself leads to failure. But when you band together with others who possess the same mindset as you—one of sacrifice, teamwork, and camaraderie—victory is inevitable. Jesus said that a house divided cannot stand (Mark 3:25). Paul admonished believers to "Strive for full restoration, encourage one another, be of one mind, live in peace. And the God of love and peace will be with you" (2 Cor. 13:11).

Joshua and the Israelites were part of a close-knit culture of people. Not only did they find strength in their numbers but they also found real value in their commitment to a common goal. They knew that success required the help of veterans who had experience in battle. They were not deterred from their mission by distractions because they rejected sin and disagreement in order to become a pure people set apart for the Lord's plan. And they united together despite ridicule, knowing that the Lord would deliver Jericho into their hands. No matter the empty words of their naysayers, God's Word surely would stand, and they would be victorious.

Joshua awoke the next morning at dawn. Having risen before everyone else, he surveyed the camp. His men gradually began to rise, rubbing the sleep from their eyes and stretching as they prepared for the fourth trek around the walls of Jericho. And that's when Joshua saw him. Eliakim was fully dressed in his armor and lacing up his sandals. Always impressed by a punctual soldier who was ready to do battle, Aryeh patted the young man's shoulder firmly as he passed by.

Eliakim looked across the camp and met Joshua's eyes. Joshua nodded at him, and Eliakim nodded back. It was as though they shared a tacit understanding that Eliakim's excursion yesterday would be a secret kept between them. Despite his fears about his inadequacy and about the future, Eliakim rightly chose to believe in the power of a people who were united in mind, heart, and mission.

Joshua gave a shout and gathered the army together. The priests and all the soldiers, including Eliakim, knew what was on the agenda for today. They didn't know for sure what the future would bring, but they were in it together.

A PRAYER FOR TODAY

Lord, I'm sorry for the times I have allowed disunity, distraction, sin, and disagreement to turn me away from Your body of believers whom You love so dearly. I know You desire that we unite with other followers of Christ on a consistent basis at church and in a small-group setting to worship You, study Your Word, grow spiritually, support each other, and hold one another accountable. Please help me to be faithful in this area and to adopt the mind of Christ. I want to value the church more than any other earthly association. I want to stand for righteousness along with Your family of believers despite mocking or persecution. Unite us, Lord, so that the world might believe! In Jesus' name I pray, amen.

THE DISCIPLINE OF CONSISTENCY

Keep putting one foot in front of the other; you're almost there!

S eth had been walking his entire life. He was born ten years in to the Israelites' forty-year trek through the wilderness and never enjoyed the stability of settling in one place for too long. As a boy, he had heard the story many times of how the elders complained and rebelled against the Lord in the wilderness after they had escaped from Egypt. They refused to believe in the power of God despite all the miraculous signs He had shown them.[1]

For this reason, they walked.

Yahweh swore to the rebels that because of their grumbling they would not see the land He had solemnly promised to their ancestors, the land flowing with milk and honey. So they moved about in the wilderness for forty years until all the men who were of military age when they left Egypt had died, since they had disobeyed the Lord. And God raised up their sons in their place.[2] Seth was a part of this new group of soldiers. When he was twenty years old, he joined the Israelite army and was determined to be more faithful than his predecessors had been.[3]

It didn't take long for Aryeh, the army's commander, to take notice of Seth's work ethic and intellect. Seth was quiet and reserved, but whenever he spoke, he possessed a rare insight that was always valuable to whatever challenge they were confronted with. He quickly rose in the ranks to become Aryeh's right-hand man. It was an honor and a privilege for Seth to serve in this way.

But having been on the move since the day he was born, Seth's spirit was unsettled. As a child, he had experienced hardship when the king of Edom denied the Israelites passage through his land and when they had to fight against the Amorites and the king of Bashan. He watched helplessly as twenty-four thousand people died from a plague because they allowed themselves to be seduced by the Moabites and they sacrificed to their gods. He traveled with his people as they camped at nearly fifty different sites after fleeing Egypt; he walked thirty years of their forty-year journey though it should only have taken them ten days to reach their destination.[4] Seth's feet had become calloused from their travels, and perhaps his heart had become somewhat hardened as well. Though walking is all he had ever known, he had grown weary of it.

As the people stood on the cusp of entering the promised land, their new leader, Joshua, told them that the Lord wanted them to walk just seven days more. Physically, it was a simple request. But mentally, it was a challenge when all they had ever done was the same thing over and over again without seeing results. Today was the fifth day of their mission to conquer the city of Jericho. Seth had to muster the will to set aside his doubts, his proven military strategy, and the discouragement from past hardships. He had to keep marching.

At dawn, Seth laced up his sandals for the umpteenth time in his life and looked around at the rest of the armed men who were doing the same. He wondered if anything would be different about this day. In two days, would God actually bring about the destruction of Jericho as He had promised? Would all his years of marching through the desert land finally come to an end? Seth stood to his feet and made his way over to Aryeh's side. The men lined up in their familiar echelon like a perfect row of grain in a bountiful field. They flanked the priests as a front and rear guard and waited for Joshua's command to descend upon Jericho for the fifth day in a row.

⤙⤚

It is said that in any great story, each scene should lead to a new question, and that we must continue reading the novel or watching the movie to discover the answer. As we read the biblical and factual story of Joshua and the Battle of Jericho, the question that comes to mind at this point in our journey is this: Will the Israelites continue to put one foot in front of the other, or will they give up right before victory out of fear, exhaustion, or frustration?

Joshua and his men had to do the same task every day for seven days. Day four required the same discipline as day one. Day five demanded the same commitment as day two. Days six and seven required the same fortitude as day four. The task may have sounded boring and the instructions may have seemed trivial or inconsequential. But the secret to most successes is doing the right thing—and doing it each and every day.

At this point in your journey to conquer the obstacles that stand in your way of victory, I want you to know that you can climb any mountain by taking one step at a time. Consistency is fundamental, and yet it's one of our biggest problems. In a world full of unlimited distractions and numerous options, consistency is one of the hardest virtues to master.

Why aren't we more consistent with our actions? Instead of putting in the time and energy necessary to achieve true success, we want fast fixes and speedy solutions. When it comes to our health, we spend money on diets and fitness plans that promise we'll lose weight quickly, even though it may have taken us years to pack on the extra girth. It's no wonder that nearly 49 percent of dieters give up after a month, according to a recent survey in the United Kingdom.[5] When it comes to our careers, 84 percent of workers in the United States and Canada are looking to quit their jobs, according to another recent study.[6] Nearly half of all students drop out of college before they've earned a degree.[7] And you've probably already heard the statistic that 40 to 50 percent of all marriages in the United States end in divorce.[8] These shocking figures demonstrate that we have become a culture of quitters.

The further along you are in your quest to cause the walls to fall down in your personal Jericho, the more you may be tempted to throw in the towel. You may begin to doubt, *Why am I doing this? Is this really going to work? Is it worth it? This is hard. It's not what I thought it would be. Nothing has changed. Things aren't getting any better, and I feel dumb for even trying. Why shouldn't I just quit right now?* But what if I told you that you were only two days, two weeks, or two short months away from victory? Would you continue to press on? Or would you decide to join the ranks of so many who choose to give up, rather than to persevere and conquer the mountains that are ready to crumble at your feet?

While consistency may not seem like the most exciting topic to discuss, I have a feeling this may end up being a favorite chapter for you. It is filled with example after example of inspiring individuals who took part in the unglamorous task of simply putting one foot in front of the other and never giving up. In doing so, they accomplished the extraordinary.

TIME IS ON YOUR SIDE

American swimmer Florence May Chadwick was the first woman to swim the English Channel in both directions. In 1950, she crossed the English Channel in thirteen hours and twenty minutes, breaking the world record. In 1951, she crossed the channel again—this time in the opposite direction, from England to France, in sixteen hours and twenty-two minutes and set yet another record.

One year later, she attempted to swim the twenty-six-mile stretch between Catalina Island and the California coastline. Small boats flanked her as she swam, with the people inside the boats, including her mother, watching out for sharks and ready to help her if she became hurt or too tired to continue. She had swum for fifteen hours when suddenly a thick fog rolled in and hovered over the water. Florence began to doubt her ability and told her mother she didn't think she could make it. She swam for another hour, but because she wasn't able to see the coastline, she asked to be pulled out of the water. Sitting in the boat, having given up on her mission, Florence learned that she had stopped swimming just one mile away from her destination.[9]

Two months later, she tried to tackle this same route once more. It must've felt like déjà vu for Florence when that thick fog rolled in again. But this time, instead of getting discouraged or doubting herself, she kept the mental image of the shoreline in her mind while she swam; and this time, she made it across.

Can you imagine swimming for fifteen to sixteen hours non-stop? I can't even comprehend swimming for one hour without resting. It's a completely different type of endurance than cycling or running, although the determination it requires is the same. To become an expert swimmer involves tremendous physical strength and stamina, breath control, and perseverance. It also involves one other element that is just as important, but might be overlooked by the average person. Swimming long distances demands a complete and total surrender to the passing of time.

When competing in any race, a person's entire goal is to finish with the best time, to be the fastest, to be the best, to break a record. But think about this for a moment: a competitor's obsession with time is not what is going to enable him or her to win. Instead, one's intense training all finally comes together, and one puts forth the very best physical effort one can muster, while being *consistent*—continuing to kick, paddle, run, or peddle, until one reaches the finish line.

Florence May Chadwick failed at her first attempt to swim from the California coast to Catalina the moment her doubts crept in, and she started thinking about how long she had already been swimming and whether or not she would actually reach her destination. She succeeded at her second attempt when she determined that despite the heavy fog and the long hours she had already been swimming, she would continue to press on until she met her goal.

On the Israelites' fifth day walking around the walls of Jericho, it may have looked as though they weren't getting anywhere, but they kept walking. They had a goal in mind, and they knew that time and the results of their obedience were in God's hands. Yet one of the biggest struggles we face as Christians is to walk by faith even when it looks as though nothing is changing. I believe the source of this problem has a lot to do with our failure to surrender to God's timing.

> ONE OF THE BIGGEST STRUGGLES WE FACE AS CHRISTIANS IS TO WALK BY FAITH EVEN WHEN IT LOOKS AS THOUGH NOTHING IS CHANGING.

In this fast-paced, technologically driven world of ours, we've gotten used to quick solutions to our problems. Are you bored? Here are six hundred television channels, myriad video games, and other activities to keep you occupied. Can't figure out a problem on your own? Here are millions of websites and mobile-phone applications from people who figured out your problem for you. (I wrote a book called *God Has an App for That!* to address this very issue.[10])

There is nothing wrong with most of these inventions in and of themselves, but the problem is that they have helped to create a culture of men and women, young and old who do not take the time to come up with new, creative solutions on their own, or put in the necessary hard work to persevere through trials in order to accomplish great things. When life gets difficult, people nowadays would rather just change the channel. Though it's natural to want pain and trials to end quickly, instant gratification doesn't teach us the virtues of patience and perseverance—nor does it teach us to learn God's lessons or to embrace His sovereign timing.

Hebrews 11 highlights certain men and women of faith in the Bible who experienced firsthand many of the trials and tribulations we face. Because they have run this spiritual race before us and prevailed, their stories serve as an encouragement to you and me to keep pushing forward.

> Therefore, since we are surrounded by such a great cloud of witnesses, let us throw off everything that hinders and the sin that so easily entangles. And let us run with perseverance the race marked out for us, fixing our eyes on Jesus, the pioneer and perfecter of faith. For the joy set before him he endured the cross, scorning its shame, and sat down at the right hand of the throne of God. Consider him who endured such opposition from sinners, so that you will not grow weary and lose heart. (Heb. 12:1–3)

Christ was a living example to us of surrender and perseverance. Romans 5:3–4 and James 1:3–4 also confirm that, like Jesus, we learn to endure through suffering and the testing of our faith. So instead of running away from trials or giving up at the first sign of trouble, we would do well to change our perspective of time and accept the opportunity to allow our heavenly Father to grow the virtue of perseverance in us.

Persevering to the point of victory takes time, and understanding that God has an eternal timetable is an important key in your walk around the daunting walls in your life.

Our Lord is the First and the Last, the Alpha and the Omega. Great theologians of old have said that He sits outside of time and space because He is eternal and Creator of all things. When I find myself becoming impatient during a particularly protracted trial or process, 2 Peter 3:8 always comes to mind: "But do not forget this one thing, dear friends: With the Lord a day is like a thousand years, and a thousand years are like a day."

God operates on a different timetable than we do. It extends beyond the years you and I will be alive on earth. Our days are few in number compared to His foreverness. Though our feeble minds cannot comprehend the length of eternity, imagine a bird disassembling the earth—twig by twig, leaf by leaf, pebble by pebble—and taking every individual element to the moon, piece by piece. After it is finished flying back and forth from the moon to the earth, and the entire earth is dissembled, eternity would just be starting.

Or envision an ant walking around and around a bowling ball until it wears down the surface of its little pathway. If the ant continued to walk until the path was disintegrated down to the center of the bowling ball so that the ball finally collapsed upon itself, it would only be a blip on the span of eternity.

Though time is incomprehensibly limitless, it is not our enemy. On the contrary, each grain of sand in our metaphorical hourglass possesses an opportunity for us to learn, to cherish, to live in the moment, and to grow as followers of Christ. Time is on your side.

When we consider the unfathomable length of eternity, it gives us a perspective that enables us to be consistent in our journey. For the

> EACH GRAIN OF SAND IN OUR METAPHORICAL HOURGLASS POSSESSES AN OPPORTUNITY FOR US TO LEARN, TO CHERISH, TO LIVE IN THE MOMENT, AND TO GROW AS FOLLOWERS OF CHRIST.

Israelites, seven days of walking around the walls of Jericho were miniscule compared to the forty years they had walked in the desert—and it was nothing compared to the measure of forever. Likewise, if you were to focus your attention on the length of eternity rather than how long you've been in the midst of your current struggle, it would help you to endure patiently. The thought of eternity makes every obstacle seem temporal and insignificant, as 2 Corinthians 4:17–18 affirms:

> For our light and momentary troubles are achieving for us an eternal glory that far outweighs them all. So we fix our eyes not on what is seen, but on what is unseen, since what is seen is temporary, but what is unseen is eternal.

Right now, commit to memory the scripture above. Seriously. Before you move on to the next section of this book, highlight or underline this verse, and repeat it as many times as you need to in order to embed the words into your heart and mind. Write it down on an index card and tape it to your bathroom mirror, the refrigerator, or the dashboard in your car. It fully and profoundly encapsulates the importance of us having the proper perspective of time related to eternity as we aim for true consistency in our walk.

BEHIND THE SCENES

I would love to see the story of Joseph made into a major motion picture someday. It is both riveting and inspiring, with a handsome leading man at the helm. There's drama, history, lust, jealousy, despair, bitterness, and revenge, and at the very end, good triumphs over evil. Joseph was a man who endured abuse, betrayal, and imprisonment, but because he woke up day after day and did the right thing despite his circumstances, God turned his tragedies into an awesome story of perseverance.

Joseph's trials began in Genesis 37, when his own brothers sold him into slavery. Not only were they jealous because their father, Jacob, favored Joseph and gave him an ornate, multicolored robe, but they also were infuriated because Joseph shared with them two different dreams he had that suggested he would rule over his family in the future. So his brothers seized an opportunity to sell him to Midianite merchants and led their father to believe that a wild animal had killed Joseph in the forest.

Joseph was then sold to Potiphar, the captain of the palace guard. The Bible says that the blessing of the Lord was upon Potiphar's house because of Joseph, so Potiphar appointed Joseph as the overseer of nearly everything he owned. But when Potiphar's wife tried to seduce Joseph and he refused her advances, she falsely accused Joseph of trying to rape her. Potiphar became furious and threw Joseph into prison.

Today, you may be feeling that there is no reward for continuing to obey the Lord and doing the right thing. Perhaps it appears that everyone else around you is doing what is wrong and getting ahead in life. Do the right thing anyway, and keep doing the right thing because there is always a short-term and a long-term result in doing what is right—just as there is a short-term and a long-term consequence for doing what is wrong. You will see how true this is as the rest of Joseph's story unfolds.

While Joseph was in prison, the Lord "showed him kindness

and granted him favor in the eyes of the prison warden. So the warden put Joseph in charge of all those held in the prison, and he was made responsible for all that was done there" (Gen. 39:21–22). The Bible says God was with Joseph even when his physical location seemed dark and hopeless. This goes to show that whenever you are fully committed to doing what is right, it doesn't matter where you might end up because God will be with you—and others will begin to notice.

Joseph's gift for interpreting dreams eventually led to his introduction to Pharaoh, the king of Egypt. And because God gave Joseph the correct interpretation of Pharaoh's dreams when everyone else had failed, Egypt was warned about a seven-year famine. Pharaoh was so impressed with Joseph's skills that he made Joseph second in command in the palace and the entire country. Joseph went throughout the land during seven years of abundance to collect and store up food, which spared the people of Egypt from starvation during the severe shortage.

In the midst of the famine, Joseph's brothers came to Egypt to seek grain. Imagine their surprise to learn that the brother they had sold into slavery was now in charge of a prosperous country! Although Joseph had every reason to exact revenge against his brothers—having suffered one harrowing ordeal after another because of their betrayal—he instead extended grace to them. Joseph offered his brothers lifesaving food at no cost and restored their broken family. He said to them, "You intended to harm me, but God intended it for good to accomplish what is now being done, the saving of many lives" (Gen. 50:20).

The story of Joseph is a huge encouragement to us today. On a deep and emotional level, it teaches us about the redeeming power of grace, hope, and forgiveness that is available to us from God at any moment. It highlights the values of perseverance and having the faith and courage to be an overcomer.

No matter what you might be going through—no matter how bad things may appear—trust that God is with you and that He is working behind the scenes on your behalf. Despite the seemingly impossible challenges you may be facing, as long as you put your trust in the Lord, you will overcome. This was true for Joseph, it was true for Joshua and the Israelites, and it is true for you.

STEP-BY-STEP

Bob Wieland is the greatest athlete I've ever had the privilege of meeting. I first heard him speak at a local high school when I was pastoring in Des Moines, Iowa, many years ago. We met at a prayer event at the state's capital sometime later. I will never forget Bob Wieland's story.

After stepping on a mortar mine in Vietnam in 1969, he lay in the jungle for five days until medics found him, declared him dead, and took him away in a body bag. Miraculously, he revived a half an hour later—almost half the man he once was, because the explosion took both of his legs. Yet Bob hasn't allowed physical limitations to stop him from achieving extraordinary feats and inspiring others to do the same. He has defied the odds as a four-time world-record holder in the bench press with a best lift of 507 pounds, although he was later disqualified because of a little-known rule in the *Lifter's Handbook* stating that competitors had to wear shoes.[11] I guess they didn't realize it's a little difficult to wear shoes if you don't have legs. Bob has also completed numerous marathons and triathlons, and in 2011, at age 65, he participated

in a solo ride across the United States and back, called the Dream
Ride 3, using a handcycle.[12]

For nearly four decades, Bob has been a sought-after motivational speaker, sharing his message of perseverance and triumph
with schools, companies, and nonprofit organizations nationwide.
I remember hearing him speak about walking across the country
on his arms. With incredible upper body strength, Bob would
plant his hands on the ground about a foot ahead of himself, and
take a step by swinging his torso forward to catch up with his
hands. He said that when he announced his cross-country goal to
the world, many people laughed at him and didn't think he'd make
it out of Los Angeles.[13] He did. Bob started in 1982, and a group of
intrigued spectators followed him. When he arrived at the Arizona
state line, they all turned back.

Bob pressed on, and the journey took him three years, eight
months, and six days.[14] He calculated that he took 4,900,000 steps
total. Bob would always ask, "Can you guess which step was the
hardest?" Then he'd answer that question with these words: "The
first one."

As Bob knows well, whether you're trying to overcome an
obstacle in your personal life or reach some type of goal, there is
no other way to begin than by taking the first step. It's a simple
principle that eludes so many. But the fact is, you could triumph
over any challenge—you could conquer an entire city—simply by
putting one foot in front of the other. That's what consistency is
all about, striving for a goal one step at a time. "Forgetting what is
behind and straining toward what is ahead, I press on toward the
goal to win the prize for which God has called me heavenward in
Christ Jesus" (Phil. 3:13–14).

Bob Wieland said that when he was in physical therapy after

the terrible incident in Vietnam, he felt insulted when the therapist handed him a five-pound weight. After all, before losing his legs he was six feet tall, 270 pounds, and an all-star athlete in college. But to his surprise, he couldn't lift the five-pound weight because he was so weak.

"That rehabilitation program was quite a journey," he said. "It certainly didn't start with the world record. It started with five pounds, but five led to ten. Ten led to fifteen. Fifteen led to twenty [and so on]."[15] After a year of intense rehabilitation, Bob moved from his hometown in Milwaukee, Wisconsin, to Southern California where he began competing against able-bodied athletes. Eight years later, he broke the official world record in the United States Powerlifting National Championships. When he was disqualified due to the shoe rule, Bob wasn't bitter about it. He told the official, "The joy had been in the journey."[16]

Bob possessed the uncommon wisdom that a journey really is just a series of steps. The journey to the promised land for the Israelites was a series of steps through the wilderness for forty years, then around the walls of Jericho for seven days. These consistent steps led to their ultimate victory, and they will do the same for you.

THOUGH YOU MAY NOT ALWAYS BE ABLE TO SEE YOUR PROGRESS, EVENTUALLY THE SUM TOTAL OF EVERY SIMPLE STEP YOU'VE TAKEN IS GOING TO RESULT IN SOMETHING TRULY WORTHWHILE.

You won't get to your destination by quitting at the first sign of trouble or getting distracted en route to your goal. With your eye on the prize, you keep walking. You persevere. You nestle the confidence deep down in your heart that, though you may not always be able to see your progress, eventually the sum total of every simple step you've taken is going to result in something truly worthwhile.

MIND GAMES

Before his career in the NBA took off, Jeremy Lin, a graduate of Harvard University, had been sleeping on his brother's couch. He had slept on his New York Knicks teammate Landry Fields's couch the night before his dreams came true and "Linsanity" swept the nation in February 2012.[17] Lin endured a series of disappointments and setbacks prior to becoming the most talked about star in basketball during the 2011–2012 season. He didn't receive a single athletic scholarship offer out of high school and was rejected by his first-choice school, Stanford University. After six months of prayer, Lin decided to enroll at Harvard, but he was not selected in the 2010 NBA draft after graduation.

Donnie Nelson, the president of basketball operations for the Dallas Mavericks, called him and reminded him that God had a perfect plan for him. "This could be just . . . another barrier that you have to overcome, but God is sovereign," Nelson told him.[18] Lin played in the NBA Summer League at Nelson's invitation and received offers to play on multiple teams such as the Dallas Mavericks, Los Angeles Lakers, and Golden State Warriors.

He chose to sign with the Warriors, which was his favorite team growing up, located in his hometown, Palo Alto, California. But Lin was released after a year without getting very many of those all-important minutes on the game clock to demonstrate his ball-handling skills. He went on to the Houston Rockets, who waived him less than a month later. The New York Knicks claimed him off waivers in December 2011. Coach Mike D'Antoni finally gave Lin a chance to play early the next year because the team was not doing well. During a game against the New Jersey Nets on February 4, 2012, Lin reached career highs, and teammate and superstar Carmelo Anthony suggested to the coach that Lin play more in the second half. According to a *Christian Post* article published that same month:

> Lin surprised everyone and became an overnight sensation when he helped secure seven consecutive wins for the Knicks. He was also the first NBA player to score at least 20 points and seven assists in each of his first four starts.
>
> "There were just so many different things that really had to happen in order for me to make it into the NBA, and you know I have a list of about twelve to fifteen things that had to happen; none of it had anything to do with me, and it was all in God's control. His fingerprints are all over my story," Lin said . . .
>
> His humility on and off the court, hard work ethic, and praises to God every chance he gets have sparked an overwhelming fan base and the subsequent "Linsanity" movement, which many hope is here to stay.[19]

Lin has shared that one of his favorite Bible verses is Romans 5:3–5:

> Not only so, but we also glory in our sufferings, because we know that suffering produces perseverance; perseverance, character; and character, hope. And hope does not put us to shame, because God's love has been poured out into our hearts through the Holy Spirit, who has been given to us.

Out of all the words in the previous verses, can you guess which word I'd like to highlight? It's not *suffering*, and it's not *perseverance*. We've already covered both of those topics. It's not *hope* or *love*, although those are two of the most significant virtues within our faith. It's the word *know*. The apostle Paul said in verses 3–4, "We also glory in our sufferings, because we *know* that suffering produces perseverance; perseverance, character; and character, hope" (emphasis added).

To be fully convinced of something in one's mind is powerful because it can motivate a person to accomplish impossible feats for the betterment of society. The Wright brothers and other aviation pioneers were convinced that it was possible for men to fly. As a result, we have the airplane that enables us to soar to great heights and travel across the world in less than a day.

The Israelites were dedicated to defeating Jericho by marching around the enormous walls of Jericho for seven days because they were convinced that the promise of God was true. Similarly, you and I must be fully convinced of God's promises and His desire to lead us to triumph in any situation we are facing. Having a razor-sharp dedication to a singular goal produces consistency. Consistency leads to victory, and victory begins in the mind.

Consider this: all the people you admire went through some kind of adversity—poverty, abuse, imprisonment for what they believed, doubt in their ability to achieve their goals, setbacks, flaky friends, or discouragement. With every awe-inspiring biography or autobiography you read, you find out what makes these extraordinary people different from every other person who has endured the same kinds of hardship. It's a steadfast determination and unwavering mind-set that they were going to change their situations, pursue their goals, and achieve them.

Choosing to focus on and believe in your success instead of succumbing to doubt and discouragement is a constant battle we all face. James 1:6–8 says this: "The one who doubts is like a wave of the sea, blown and tossed by the wind. That person should not expect to receive anything from the Lord. Such a person is double-minded and unstable in all they do." This verse comes while James was talking specifically about persevering under trial and receiving wisdom in the midst of those trials. I believe the apostle hit on single-mindedness in this specific context because of its impact on our perseverance. Having a singular, laserlike focus on a goal helps people maintain consistency. But a person with a mixed-up mentality is like a man trying to run both north and south at the same time. He will only be in conflict with himself and end up going nowhere.

Jeremy Lin's commitment to his basketball dream is impressive, but of greater worth is his eternal mission. Every morning when he wakes up, he reminds himself that he's not playing for anything on this earth, but for his prize in heaven—for the upward call that Paul talked about. I love what he shared during an interview with GoodTV, a Taiwanese evangelical Christian channel. He said, "The Bible talks a lot about how God takes bad situations . . . and He teaches us, and He uses those times of suffering to draw us closer to him. And that's what I try to focus on during those times. For me, when I get knocked down, I really try to get back up and go at it again. I don't like to give up."[20]

TEN THOUSAND HOURS

According to author and speaker Malcolm Gladwell, it takes ten thousand hours to become phenomenal at anything. In his bestselling book *Outliers*, he examined the factors that contribute to high levels of success in men and women who do things that are out of the ordinary. He looked at the lives of geniuses, business tycoons, rock stars, and other world-class experts.

Gladwell found that by age twenty, elite violinists had logged ten thousand hours of practice each. He also discovered that to become a chess grand master, it takes about ten years—equivalent to ten thousand hours—of hard practice. Before legendary rock group the Beatles came to America in 1964 and took the world by storm, they were the house band for a small club in Hamburg, Germany, playing eight-hour sets, seven days a week, for months at a time. They had an incredibly long season of apprenticeship, when their taste and excellence in music became more and more advanced, and yet many of us think of them as overnight successes.[21]

How many of us are willing to put in the time to endure hardship and testing in order to become extraordinary at something? How many of us are willing to spend countless hours in a gym taking shots well into the night as Michael Jordan was known to have done? The phrase, "practice makes perfect" would be better stated, "perseverance makes perfect." That's because everyone who has ever been great at anything has had to consistently persevere through challenges and hardships.

I'm sure there had to be a moment when John, Paul, George, and Ringo doubted that they'd ever make it out of that low-paying gig in Hamburg and catch their big break. Michael Jordan, arguably the best basketball player of all time, tried out for the basketball team in his sophomore year of high school and did not make the cut.[22] But consistency means continuing to press on toward a goal, unthwarted. It means getting up every day and doing the right thing, logging the hours, and patiently striving to become better.

Do you remember Baruch from day 3 of our journey? He was the guy whom the Bible says *zealously* laid brick after brick during the rebuilding of the walls of Jerusalem. Not only was Baruch able to find holiness, honor, and joy in his job, but he also put in the time necessary to cultivate consistency. So is the person who stays at the bedside of an ailing or aging loved one, and the one who is faithful in a marriage year after year throughout all the highs and lows, and the missionary who continues to serve the poor in underdeveloped countries without glory or fanfare.

> CONSISTENCY MEANS GETTING UP EVERY DAY AND DOING THE RIGHT THING, LOGGING THE HOURS, AND PATIENTLY STRIVING TO BECOME BETTER.

And the marathon runner. If you've ever trained for a marathon, you know how grueling it can be on the body. If it were easy, runners wouldn't get a medal at the end. Training requires many exhausting hours of running and conditioning the body in order to make it the full 26.2 miles. Little by little, a few miles a day turns into a marathon of hard work, difficulty, and sacrifice.

Tony Robbins is a motivational guru who has made a fortune trying to get people to identify a goal and to do something every day—no matter how small—to reach that goal. He's teaching people to be consistent, and that's why Tony Robbins and many of his followers have been successful. To actively and continuously work toward overcoming obstacles in life is a skill like any other, and having the wisdom to make good decisions and to follow God's will takes time and experience to develop.

Embrace the daily struggle, knowing that you're accruing valuable hours that are making you stronger, better, and wiser to deal with grander problems afflicting our world. Don't give up. Victory is coming—it's just around the corner. But you must persevere.

JUST FOR TODAY

Perhaps you can relate to King David in Psalm 6:3–4: "My soul is in deep anguish. How long, LORD, how long? Turn, LORD, and deliver me; save me because of your unfailing love." Sometimes it may seem as though we will never obtain victory over an impossible obstacle in our lives, or that our deliverance is never going to come. But Galatians 6:9 instructs us: "Let us not grow weary in doing good, for at the proper time we will reap a harvest if we do not give up."

A farmer wakes up at the first light of day to conduct the tedious work of tilling the soil and nurturing various crops in order to reap a harvest. He works until the sun dips beneath the horizon and patiently waits for those first curled green leaves to emerge from the ground, giving way to healthy, edible delights. The farmer endures drought, scorching sun, storms, and seasons when the land seems barren. He puts in the hard work now and perseveres in order to reap benefits in the future.

Many of us aren't familiar with the concept of a farmer striving to harvest his or her provisions. I think part of the reason is because hot and fully prepared food is available to us instantaneously. Did you know in our country today there are approximately 160,000 fast-food establishments?[23] If you want a juicy hamburger for lunch or a delicious burrito at midnight, it's yours in a matter of minutes. But in biblical times, some farmers lived hand to mouth. They would depend on every single harvest. Without a good harvest, they could face severe hunger or even starvation. If they didn't persevere, they wouldn't eat. What if we, like the farmer, focused solely on the hard work of today?

Shepherd Church has a ministry called Christ Powered Recovery, or CPR, to serve men and women who have been adversely affected by alcohol and/or drugs. Whenever I hear that name, I imagine people whose lives have been nearly destroyed by the tornado of addiction, being brought back to life through CPR. The ministry welcomes anyone who has a desire to stay clean and sober by surrendering his or her addiction to Jesus Christ.

My dear friend Mike, along with a guy named Jeff, founded the ministry several years back. Mike had been a basketball coach at the college level, suffered from a kidney stone, and was given a prescription for painkillers by his doctor. As you might've already guessed, it didn't take long for my friend to become addicted to the painkillers. At one time, he was taking the equivalent of sixty Vicodin a day—a grave addiction he managed to keep hidden from his wife, children, and colleagues.

Relentlessly, he searched high and low for ways to obtain more pills. He became unfocused and depressed. He constantly lied to cover his tracks. His marriage was on the rocks, and he knew it. His career was in jeopardy due to his erratic behavior. Our church's executive pastor, Tim Winters, finally sat Mike down in his office and confronted him about what he suspected, but Mike vehemently denied everything and walked out the door. Having officially hit rock bottom, Mike drove to the parking lot of a country club, placed a loaded .38-caliber pistol in his mouth, and pulled the trigger. Inexplicably, apart from the grace of God, the gun did not fire. Seconds later, Mike's phone rang. It was Tim asking if he was okay. Mike broke down and confessed everything. He surrendered his life to Jesus Christ and got clean through a seventeen-day stay in detox and a twelve-step program with the support of his faithful wife and the church community. Two years later, he cofounded Christ Powered Recovery at our church.

God restored Mike's life, marriage, family, and career. He shares with anyone who will listen that recovery is a constant battle. He said, "You don't have to worry about staying clean and sober for the rest of your life; you just have focus on being clean and sober *today*."

This is the same motto we should have in our battles with any other foe in our lives. Sometimes we look too far into the future, and we think, *There's no way I can keep up this fight for another day, week, month, or year.* Yet Jesus told us not to worry about tomorrow because it has enough trouble of its own (Matt. 6:34). In fact, He also told us not to look back at the past (Luke 9:61–62). You can't march forward with confidence and purpose while at the same time looking backward. It's just not possible.

If your problem is weight loss, all you have to worry about is making healthy choices for today. If you are grappling with a strained marriage or rebellious children, you don't need to become overwhelmed by the future; you simply need enough patience, wisdom, and grace for today. If you're not sure what will happen with your job or schooling, endeavor to do your best today and cast all your concerns about tomorrow unto the Lord (1 Peter 5:7).

Jesus imparted great freedom to us when he said in Matthew 6:25–27:

> Therefore I tell you, do not worry about your life, what you will eat or drink; or about your body, what you will wear. Is not life more than food, and the body more than clothes? Look at the

birds of the air; they do not sow or reap or store away in barns, and yet your heavenly Father feeds them. Are you not much more valuable than they? Can any one of you by worrying add a single hour to your life?

One important key to consistency is focusing solely on today, knowing that God will provide everything you need. He has today, tomorrow, and the rest of our lives covered. Therefore, we can rest assured that the sum total of keeping the faith today, persevering today, and doing the right thing today, eventually equals consistent behavior that results in victory. It's like hammering away at a wall, bit by bit, until the wall falls down. We need not worry about tomorrow or ask, "How long, Lord?" We need only to be concerned with today.

Here's a quick activity for you to do right now. Take a moment to figure out how many waking hours are left today. Are there eight hours left today? Three and a half? Two? However much time is left today—this day—resolve to do what's right in the eyes of God. Whether it's making a conscious decision to set aside your fear and worry and to trust in the Lord or extending forgiveness and grace to someone in your life, do the right thing with the time you have left today. You simply may need to open your Bible and spend some time in God's Word, reading and praying. You may need to turn off the television and shut down the Internet.

Pray and ask God what needs to be cleaned up in your life today and what He would like you to do in order

> YOU NEVER HAVE TO FEEL AS THOUGH ANY DAY IS RUINED. THE MIRACLE OF "TODAY" IS THAT IT CAN BE REDEEMED AT A MOMENT'S NOTICE.

to please Him. I'm confident He will make it very clear to you, and when He does, determine to do those things with the remaining time you have left today. This is a simple exercise you can do at any time, any day of the week—even if you feel as if the entire day has been a mess and you've made mistake after mistake. You can stop and figure out how much time you have left and start over from that point forward. You can commit to serving the Lord and living for the Lord with your remaining time. You never have to feel as though any day is ruined. The miracle of today is that it can be redeemed at a moment's notice.

CAN YOU SEE THE RESULTS?

When I was fifteen years old, my grandmother opened a savings account for me. She didn't have much; she just knew the value of saving and passed that legacy on to me. A strong, yet gentle woman with grace and wisdom in her sparkling eyes, my grandmother shared the eighty-ten-ten rule with me at a young age, and I've followed it ever since. The rule is really a financial planning guide. You give 10 percent of your income to the Lord (as the Bible instructs us to do in Leviticus 27:30–33 and Malachi 3:10); you put another 10 percent in savings, and you live off the remaining 80 percent.

I'm so thankful that my grandmother shared the eighty-ten-ten principle with me. Since I was a young teenager, it didn't matter if I had received fifty cents or fifty dollars; I have always given 10 percent to God, saved 10 percent, and lived off the rest. If you are not familiar with this guide or have not subscribed to it, think back over your life and imagine if you always had saved a dime out of every dollar that made its way to your hands. How much money would you have saved today?

This principle definitely goes against our culture that tells us to spend, spend, spend. It's a culture that convinces us we need to have the latest and greatest tools and technology, fashions and fads, exotic vacations and impressive cars that depreciate the moment you drive them off the lot. Besides the occasional television commercial with a voice-over from a rugged, cowboy-sounding guy who tells us to invest wisely, we really don't get very many messages from our culture that praise the value of saving. And we certainly don't see or hear any messages, apart from at church, that instruct us to give God a small portion of our incomes.

The reality is that most twenty- and thirtysomethings aren't thinking about socking away for retirement or unexpected medical bills. Instead, many people live paycheck to paycheck as rent, food, cable, car payments, gas, clothing, and entertainment take up their entire incomes, leaving nothing left for the Lord or a savings account. I wish my grandmother were alive today to explain the eighty-ten-ten rule to everyone who would lend an ear. I wonder how many people would be attentive to her wisdom and be able to envision the big results that come from little decisions such as saving and tithing each week.

A quote often attributed to Winston Churchill reads, "However beautiful the strategy, you should occasionally look at the results."[24] When you and I visualize the end results of our hard work, it enables us to consistently make important sacrifices and to persevere. This is the final key to consistency I'd like to share with you, and it's essential to your overall victory.

You will find the daily strength you need to raise your child in a godly manner when you visualize the result of your efforts—a future adult who loves the Lord and who strives to use his or her time and talent to make the world a better place. You will muster the courage you need to weather the storms of your life when you can see the results of your endurance—becoming a person of faith who trusts in God and believes joy comes in the morning. You will glean the grace you need to keep praying for and showing love to a seemingly indifferent spouse when you recognize the results of your faithfulness—a marriage restored by God's grace.

On the fifth day of the Israelites' mission, the task of marching around Jericho's perimeter could only have been propelled by their focus on the results God promised them. You, too, can successfully maintain consistency by zeroing in on the results of your hard work. This seemingly small, daily decision will lead to victory in whatever battle you are facing personally.

For five days, can you find a quiet place and have a morning devotional, knowing that your quiet time with the Lord will result in your heart being cleansed, challenged, and renewed? If weight loss is your constant battle, can you find an hour a day for five consecutive days to engage in an exercise you enjoy, be it hiking, walking, jogging, biking, dancing, or going to the gym? If your obstacle is a conflict with a loved one or a coworker, can you get down on your knees and pray sincerely for five days that your heart as well as your foe's will be softened by God's love and grace? Can you commit to going to church with your family for five continuous weekends, or tithing 10 percent of your income for five consecutive paychecks, or kissing your wife goodbye and telling her you love her five mornings in a row, or praying with your spouse and/or your children for five days straight?

It has been said that it takes sixty-six days to either form or break a habit, but all I am asking you to do is be consistent for five days in a row.[25] See what happens. Every day put one foot in front of the other. Start small and keep it up, visualizing the results of your hard work. Before you know it, you will have formed a positive behavior, routine, or mind-set that will be crucial in making your impossible walls fall down.

———

Seth looked up at the massive stones composing the walls of Jericho as he followed a circuit that had become all too familiar over the past week. Each boulder was at least the size of his torso. If one of them should fall from its unyielding position and land on him or another soldier, he most certainly would be crushed to death. And that was just one stone. The entire first wall was indeed a force to be reckoned with. How was it possible that their small steps could bring down this impossible obstacle?

Seth suddenly heard Joshua's voice beside him. "A good soldier is faithful and consistent," Joshua said. "He marches step-by-step and is not easily thwarted. He never gives up. You're an excellent soldier, Seth."

"Thank you, sir," Seth replied, taken aback by the unexpected compliment.

Earlier that morning, weariness and doubt had shaken Seth's commitment to pursue the goal set before him and the Israelites. But as he marched beneath the shadow of these imposing walls, he knew there was nothing else he could do except what he had always done—walk.

Israel has walked for forty years and five days to get to this moment, he thought. *Surely I can walk for two more days.* So Seth resolved that he would continue to walk until he saw victory.

A PRAYER FOR TODAY

Almighty God, You are so consistent in Your faithful love toward us. You are always working behind the scenes for our benefit, and yet we are so inconsistent. Please help me to walk by faith, putting one foot in front of the other, even when it looks as though nothing is changing. Remind me that You have an eternal timetable that is different from mine. Every hour, day, month, or year I wait to seize the victory, I pray that I would embrace the opportunity to grow in patience and perseverance through the journey—being fully convinced that You will deliver on Your promises. Please give me enough grace and strength for today. In Jesus' name I pray, amen.

OBEDIENCE BRINGS THE BLESSINGS

Follow God's instructions every step of the way.

Something was different about the soldiers today as they marched around the walls of Jericho. Though they walked with the same quietness and resolve, there was an unmistakable eagerness in their steps. They looked as though they were chomping at the bit like bridled horses, or prideful young lions ready to pounce upon their prey. Joshua noticed it. Caleb noticed it. Aryeh noticed it. And Seth noticed it. The four men looked at one another, their eyes communicating an unspoken concern about this new hunger the men were exhibiting. With each step, the tension grew.

When Joshua was a boy, he and Caleb had a favorite game they would play with their friends. The rules were clear and simple: Two friends got less than a minute to hide together someplace in the camp, and the objective of the other friends was to set out and find them. If the hiders were found, they had to be the seekers in the next round. If they went undetected, they were the winners and got to hide again. One day, a boy named Gil was on Joshua's team. None of the older boys ever wanted to be Gil's partner because he was a few years younger and full of loud, unrestrained energy and exuberance.

"Listen. If you want to win, you need to do exactly as I say," Joshua told Gil sternly before the game started. "When it's our turn to hide, I'm going to find a good spot, so be quick and follow me wherever I go. Don't dillydally. And be quiet. Do you understand?"

Gil nodded eagerly. So when it was time for Caleb and another lad to be the seekers, they counted to fifty and Joshua and Gil took off running. Joshua grabbed Gil's hand and pulled him beneath a table where some women were preparing manna into delicious, little flat cakes. The table had a cloth over it that went almost to the ground. It was the perfect place to conceal them.

"Forty-eight, forty-nine, fifty!" they heard Caleb's call from the other side of camp.

Gil began to giggle.

Joshua shoved Gil's shoulder in hopes of snapping him out of his silly mood.

But when they heard Caleb and his partner coming closer, Gil's entire body began to shake as he attempted to hold back his excitement. The suspense was all too much for him, so Joshua covered Gil's mouth with his hand.

"If you laugh, they're going to find us," Joshua whispered, "and then we'll lose."

Caleb's footsteps could be heard shuffling in the dirt nearby. They came closer and closer to the table, paused for a moment, and then turned in the opposite direction. After a minute or two, the coast was clear. Joshua removed his hand from over Gil's mouth.

"We did it!" Gil exclaimed.

Joshua rolled his eyes. He would have been better off having a wild goat for a partner. Just then, the tablecloth flew open, and there was Caleb with a huge grin on his face.

Flash forward to present day. No longer fun and games, the stakes had never been higher for Joshua and his comrades. He wondered if the men were about to ruin the mission as Gil did when they were children because he just couldn't contain himself.

It takes a special kind of maturity to exercise patience and precisely obey God's instructions. Because of the tension, Joshua was unsure the soldiers would be up for the challenge. But to his relief, the armed men and the priests completed their one revolution around the city of Jericho for the sixth day in a row, and then headed back to camp. That's when Eliakim broke the silence.

"I don't understand why we need to wait another day," he said. "Why can't we turn back right now and storm the city? Why are we waiting? We're ready *today*!"

Half of the men roared in agreement with Eliakim, raising their spears and other weapons in the air. Aryeh, who had been walking with Joshua, Caleb, and Seth ahead of the group, turned on his heel to face the soldiers.

"*Silence!*" he shouted.

The raucous noise quickly reduced to a small murmur. Then complete silence. Aryeh walked through the crowd as it parted easily for him. None of the men dared to look him in the eye lest he be devoured by his anger. Aryeh stopped when he came to the undersized soldier who had just spoken such oversized words.

"Eliakim, son of Yigal, how do you suggest that we storm the city?" Aryeh asked him.

Eliakim tried to stand a little taller, but he did not reply.

The commander continued, "The gates are securely barred. Do you suggest we run through them? Your thick-headedness *might* be able to make a dent in the iron, but that won't do us much good. Or perhaps we spend the next three months digging underneath the first wall and then another three months digging underneath the second wall? Shall we scale to the top of walls that are at least five times your height? Or perhaps we sprout wings and fly over or bang on the front gate and politely ask the men of Jericho to let us in?"

Eliakim shifted eye contact from Aryeh's steely gaze and looked down at the rust-colored soil at his feet. The other men chuckled.

"Are the commands of the Lord a laughing matter?" Joshua asked them.

He made his way through the path in the middle of the crowd and stood next to Aryeh.

"God told us specifically how He would deliver Jericho into our hands, and it seems you all need a reminder," Joshua continued. "The Lord said that we, along with the priests, are to march around the city once a day for six days. On the seventh day, we are to march around the city seven times, with the priests blowing the trumpets. Eliakim, what day is it today?"

"It's the sixth day, sir," Eliakim answered sheepishly.

"That is correct," Joshua said. "You are not to give a war

cry or raise your voices until the time tomorrow in which I tell you to shout. We must obey the Word of God. Only then will we receive the blessing of our inheritance."

⤙⤚

God asked the Israelites to march around the walls of Jericho once a day for six consecutive days. They did. He told them that on the seventh day they were to march around the walls seven times, and they did. Then He said they were to shout as loudly as they could when they heard the priests sound the trumpets. They did this too. None of these instructions made sense, but during this particular battle God's people chose to obey. And the Lord brought about a victory that has echoed throughout the ages. The impossible became the possible.

Herein lies the secret to our successes.

It wasn't prayer or fasting that brought about this uncommon victory, although prayer and fasting are indispensable commands that every believer should heed. It wasn't the cleverness, military tactics, or strength of the Israelites. It was the power and blessing of God—unleashed by the faith and obedience of His people.

You see, if the Lord had elected to, He could have snapped His fingers and made the walls fall down without requiring any effort at all from His people. But I believe God chose an unconventional plan to not only confuse the enemy but also test the Israelites' faith—to see if they would obey Him. Would the Lord's people do exactly as

> IT WAS THE POWER AND BLESSING OF GOD— UNLEASHED BY THE FAITH AND OBEDIENCE OF HIS PEOPLE.

He instructed, or would they adjust the plans to make them more palatable?

We're good at that, aren't we? We will take the Ten Commandments and turn them into the Ten Suggestions. We'll doctor them up until they fit our lifestyles. We will pick and choose the words of Jesus we're most comfortable with and live out a cushy Christianity. But, as Saint Augustine wrote, "If you believe what you like in the gospels, and reject what you don't like, it is not the gospel you believe, but yourself."[1]

After the Israelites had marched around the city once, absolutely nothing happened. They went around a second time, and still nothing. After the third time, there wasn't the tiniest tremor or even the smallest inkling that those walls were going to budge. So they could have decided, "You know, let's not get all legalistic about what God may or may not have said. We don't need to be so technical about the number of days we're supposed to walk around these walls. Let's just wear our camouflage gear and take the city by surprise tomorrow night!"

If the priests and soldiers had chosen to alter or abridge God's plan in any way, shape, or form, they would have failed miserably. Period. The Lord had brought them to an impossible situation that only He could get them through. It would be His way or no other way at all. The point is that God has a plan, and He doesn't want His plan tampered with. Instead, He invites willing and obedient people to carry out His plan.

God had a plan to create a vast nation through a baby He gave to Abraham and Sarah, even though they were very old at the time their son, Isaac, was born. God had a plan to turn fishermen into fishers of men called the twelve disciples. He had a plan to send His Son, not as a king but as a carpenter, to save the world. The Bible says the Lord's ways are not our ways and that He has "chosen the foolish things of the world to confound the wise" (Isa. 55:8; 1 Cor. 1:27 KJV). And as we discussed in day 2, God's plan may not always make sense, but our job is simply to obey His plan. Why, then, do we disobey?

DISSECTING DISOBEDIENCE

The Israelites' journey from Egypt to Jericho had been characterized by many ups and downs. Miracles were followed by praise and celebration. But soon deliverance was supplanted by disbelief, doubt, and fear. Moments of uncertainty resulted in complaining and grumbling. Their leader, Moses, went up to Mount Sinai for forty days to converse with the Lord, and do you know what the people did while he was gone? They engaged in revelry and idolatry. They molded a golden calf and worshiped it as a god.

When you think about it, each of us has his or her own golden calf. It's a symbol of disobedience—that thing we are tempted to worship, trust, and idolize when we feel God is far off or that He can't see us. That thing we set upon a throne that should only be occupied by God Almighty. It could be our wealth, careers, relationships, sex, drugs, alcohol, food, celebrities, hobbies, fashion, or technology. To worship a created thing is the same kind of idolatry the Israelites engaged in as they waited for Moses to return from Mount Sinai.

God will not share the throne of your heart with anything or anyone. Our flesh, which is always in competition with our spirit

(Gal. 5:16–17), tries to convince us that no one will ever find out if we engage in sinful behavior. But the Bible says that nothing is hidden from the Lord (Luke 8:17; Heb. 4:13).

Do you know what the devil's number-one trick is? It's getting you to believe that there will not be a consequence to your sin. One of the biggest lies perpetuated in our world today is that we can do whatever we want as long as no one gets hurt. But when we disobey God, someone *always* gets hurt. After the golden-calf incident, a severe plague came upon the Israelites, and many people suffered because of it. While it may not be immediate in every case, there is always a consequence to disobedience. And as Pastor Rick Warren has said, "A sin may be private, but it's never strictly personal. It affects others whether you know it or not."[2]

> ONE OF THE BIGGEST LIES PERPETUATED IN OUR WORLD TODAY IS THAT WE CAN DO WHATEVER WE WANT AS LONG AS NO ONE GETS HURT. BUT WHEN WE DISOBEY GOD, SOMEONE *ALWAYS* GETS HURTS.

I believe our sinful, human tendency toward disobedience is one of the reasons God chose to give His people such unusual instructions for Jericho's defeat. He had to bring the Israelites to the end of themselves. By carrying out His unconventional plan, God's people would be forced to set aside their trust in themselves, the things fashioned by their own hands, and their own power and cleverness. By the time they had completed their seventh trip around the walls on the seventh day, the Israelites would realize their victory would come only from God—that He is sovereign and powerful and the Lord God Jehovah-jireh, which means "The LORD Will Provide" (Gen. 22:14).

God always has our best interests in mind. He wants us to obey Him because He loves us and desires that our lives bring Him glory. Like a good parent, the Lord asks us to respect and honor His rules so that we will be safe and have the best life possible. So the question remains: why do we disobey God so often and so willingly? Allow me to share with you several answers that will help us get to the root of disobedience.

1. THE HEART IS DECEITFUL.

How many times in your life have you been encouraged to follow your heart when you were faced with a difficult decision? While the heart enables us to experience noble virtues such as love and compassion, it is far from an accurate moral compass. Do you know what the Bible says about the heart? It's pretty startling. Take a look at Jeremiah 17:9–10:

> *The heart is deceitful above all things,*
> *And desperately wicked;*
> *Who can know it?*
> *I, the LORD, search the heart,*
> *I test the mind,*
> *Even to give every man according to his ways,*
> *According to the fruit of his doings.* (NKJV)

Unfortunately, our actions are often the result of our feelings. But when we do whatever our hearts dictate in the moment, it leads to disaster. After Moses and Joshua went up to Mount Sinai for their forty-day visit with God, the people began to feel as though their leader would never return. They told Aaron, Moses' brother, to fashion the golden calf for them so that it could be their god.

Once the idol had been molded, they shouted and sang and danced around it, doing what felt good to them at the time instead of obeying God's first and second commandments (Ex. 20:3–4).

Like them, our culture believes that life is one big party and adjusts its morals by its feelings. If lying or cheating or stealing or premarital sex or holding a grudge sits well with us, no problem! We justify our actions by saying, "Hey, everyone else is doing it!"

As I write, the aftermath of the Lance Armstrong doping scandal has erupted in the media. The US Anti-Doping Agency convicted the professional road-racing cyclist of using performance-enhancing drugs. Armstrong was then stripped of his seven Tour de France titles and banned from cycling. Major League Baseball and other sports have had their own sets of issues with steroid use. So why do these popular athletes risk everything by disobeying the rules?

Lance Armstrong confessed that he used drugs because everyone else was using. He said there was no way he could compete and win if he didn't do the same. I read the other day, "Of the 21 top three finishers in the Tour de France during Lance Armstrong's victory streak, only one has not been tied to doping, according to the U.S. Anti-Doping Agency."[3]

> JOSHUA AND THE ISRAELITES UNDERSTOOD THERE WERE NO SHORTCUTS IN GOD'S PLAN.

The epidemic of cheating in the sport of cycling mirrors the same struggles we average folks face. We disobey God's commands and the laws of the land all the time because everyone else is doing it. We think everyone else is having sex outside of marriage, drinking excessively, flying down the freeway well above the speed limit, or lying on taxes, so we follow suit. We start to believe there is no other way to get ahead in this world than to cheat as well.

I believe Joshua and the Israelites understood there were no shortcuts in God's plan. They didn't rush through the task or skip a day. They didn't employ their own tactics such as digging underneath the walls or inventing dynamite or a catapult system. They simply obeyed the command of the Lord, trusting that He was going to do what He said He would do. They knew God was in control. This brings us to the second source of disobedience.

2. WE WANT TO BE IN CONTROL.

Mankind is perpetually engaged in a struggle to control our own lives. No one likes to be told what to do. Even Christians have difficulty surrendering control to God. Many of us will pray, "Lord, here is my plan. Bless it." But the Lord is looking for people whose sincere prayer will be, "God, what is *Your* plan? Whatever it is, I will obey!"

As Jesus agonized in the Garden of Gethsemane about the terrible things that were about to happen to Him, He "fell with his face to the ground and prayed, 'My Father, if it is possible, may this cup be taken from me. Yet not as I will, but as you will'" (Matt. 26:39). Then He surrendered control of His life to God—actually giving up His life through His death on the cross. Because of Christ's selfless submission to the Father's will, you and I reap the benefits of forgiveness and a direct relationship with God.

Thankfully, the disciples also surrendered control of their lives and were obedient to the commission Jesus laid out in Matthew 28:16–20. As a result, the Holy Spirit was unleashed upon believers, and innumerable souls across generations, cultures, races, and languages have been saved for the kingdom of God ever since.

3. FEAR MISLEADS US.

The final reason we disobey the Lord's commands is because of fear and lack of trust in God. You would think that our love and respect for God would motivate us to obey Him, but that is not always the case. Sometimes we're afraid of what will happen to us if we step out in faith. We're afraid of change, the unknown, and what God might possibly lead us to do if we obey.

Joyce Meyer exposed the true motivation of fear when she wrote, "Remember that any time you try to obey God, any time you try to step out into something you have never done before, any time you start trying to come out of a bondage you have worked yourself into, fear will rush right up in your face and try to stop you."[4]

Don't allow fear to rob you of the value of a deeper relationship with the Lord and the joy of obtaining ultimate victory. Though obedience is not always easy, know that the road to disobedience is much tougher, and littered with the tears and heavy steps of those who failed to follow God's road map.

Blessings are in store for those who trust and obey the Lord. This is a powerful principle we see over and over again in Jesus' ministry here on earth. Let's take a look at a few compelling examples.

THE REAL JESUS

Many people like to think of Jesus as a warm and fuzzy guy, who only went around healing people and saying nice things such as, "Love your neighbor as yourself" (Mark 12:31). We like to picture the Jesus who welcomed and blessed the little children, but not so much the Jesus who overturned the sellers' tables in God's holy temple out of righteous anger. I hear the message repeated frequently in our culture that since Jesus hung out with tax collectors and sinners, He wouldn't judge the sins of people today. It is true that Jesus showed love and compassion to the outcasts of society, but over and over again in the Gospels we see Him beckoning people to leave their sins behind and follow Him.

Though well-meaning people have reduced the mission of Christ simply to feeding the poor, healing the sick, and being kind to the hurting, this assessment is not completely accurate. His ministry certainly was filled with many acts of love and kindness, but Jesus also unequivocally called people to repent and to obey the commands of God (Matt. 5:17–19). In his book, *Obeying Jesus: The Seven Commands for Every Disciple*, Steve DuPlessie wrote:

> IT IS TRUE THAT JESUS SHOWED LOVE AND COMPASSION TO THE OUTCASTS OF SOCIETY, BUT OVER AND OVER AGAIN IN THE GOSPELS WE SEE HIM BECKONING PEOPLE TO LEAVE THEIR SINS BEHIND AND FOLLOW HIM.

The whole Sermon on the Mount in Matthew chapters 5–7 is one long list of Do's and Don'ts: "Do not resist an evil person. If someone strikes you on the right cheek, turn to him the other also." "Love your enemies and pray for those who persecute you . . ." And on it goes.

In fact, if you take some time to read through the four gospels—Matthew, Mark, Luke and John—you'll notice that Jesus gave a *lot* of commands. Commands about how to live, how to act, how to spend your money, how to think, how to worship.[5]

Not the tolerant and easygoing guy He is often made out to be, Jesus asks His followers to do many things. But I am convinced He wants to bless us when we obey Him, just as a good father would want to bless his children (Luke 11:11–13). And as a father who is not only good but also wise, the Lord often waits to see if we will follow His instructions before He disperses the blessing. We see examples of this throughout the Bible.

Take, for instance, the ten lepers in Luke 17:11–19. As Jesus was going into a village near the border between Samaria and Galilee, on His way to Jerusalem, ten men who had leprosy saw their once-in-a-lifetime opportunity to receive miraculous healing. They called out to Him, "Jesus, Master, have pity on us!" (v. 13).

Verse 14 tells us that when the Lord saw these ten lepers and heard their plea, "He said, 'Go, show yourselves to the priests.' And as they went, they were cleansed."

I am certain that Jesus could have blessed these men with healing right there and then. After all, He had done this many times throughout the Scriptures. But in this particular situation, He wanted the lepers to do something first. Christ told them to go and show themselves to the priests, as was the custom in the Levitical law when a person was healed of leprosy. And as they went—as they obeyed what Jesus commanded them to do—they were healed. The lepers obeyed, and *then* the Lord blessed them.

We find another great example in the story of the blind man in John 9:1–12. During His travels, Jesus encountered a man who had been blind since birth. Having pity on the man, the Lord spit on the ground, creating a kind of paste with mud and saliva, and put the mixture on the man's eyes. (You might be thinking, *Ewww, that's gross!* But I'll tell you, that was some holy spit and mud right there.) Then Jesus said to the blind man, "Go, wash in the Pool of Siloam" (v. 7).

Again, Jesus was asking the man to do something first, and the Bible says, "So the man went and washed, and came home seeing" (v. 7). Just like the ten lepers, the blind man obeyed the command of the Lord and received the blessing of healing.

Obedience ushered in the blessings.

Now you may be thinking, *Wait a minute, Dudley. It sounds like you're talking about that works-based salvation stuff. It's all about our faith in God, not our obedience.* No, I'm talking about the relationship between our obedience and the blessings of the Lord. It is true that each of these men demonstrated he had put his faith in Jesus, and faith is very important. In fact, Hebrews 11:6 says that without faith, it's impossible to please God—but the second half of that verse also states that God "*rewards* those who earnestly seek him" (emphasis added).

Faith and obedience go hand in hand, just as James, the brother of Jesus, asserted in James 2:17–18, 20–24:

> In the same way, faith by itself, if it is not accompanied by action, is dead.
>
> But someone will say, "You have faith; I have deeds."
>
> Show me your faith without deeds, and I will show you my faith by my deeds. . . .
>
> You foolish person, do you want evidence that faith without deeds is useless? Was not our father Abraham considered righteous for what he did when he offered his son Isaac on the altar? You see that his faith and his actions were working together, and his faith was made complete by what he did. And the scripture was fulfilled that says, "Abraham believed God,

and it was credited to him as righteousness," and he was called God's friend. You see that a person is considered righteous by what they do and not by faith alone.

James chose the excellent Old Testament example of Abraham to demonstrate his point. In Genesis 22, God told Abraham to sacrifice his only son, Isaac, on a mountain. The Bible doesn't say that Abraham argued with God, questioned Him, or disobeyed, but he got up "early the next morning" (v. 3) and set out for the region of Moriah with his son, two servants, a donkey, and enough wood for the burnt offering. You probably know the rest of this story—that Abraham obeyed God to the point of laying Isaac upon an altar and raising his knife to slay him, when an angel of the Lord called to him from heaven and stopped him. Pay close attention to what the angel said next:

> "I swear by myself, declares the LORD, that because you have done this and have not withheld your son, your only son, *I will surely bless you* and make your descendants as numerous as the stars in the sky and as the sand on the seashore. Your descendants will take possession of the cities of their enemies, and through your offspring all nations on earth *will be blessed, because you have obeyed me.*" (vv. 16–18, emphasis added)

Abraham was blessed because he obeyed God—and God promised that all nations on earth would be blessed *because* of Abraham's obedience. As you walk around the walls of your personal Jericho, remember the words of Jesus and the examples of the ten lepers, the blind man at the Pool of Siloam, and Abraham. Obedience always brings blessings.

TWO KINDS OF BLESSINGS

Who doesn't want to be blessed? I bet if you stood in the middle of Times Square in New York City and asked a thousand people if they wanted to be blessed—to be content and to have goodness bestowed on their lives—not a single person would say no. Psalm 1 provides a wealth of insight about how we can be blessed, outlining the rewards of obedience and the consequences of disobedience. This first chapter in the book of Psalms paints two different pictures for us: a picture of true wisdom and a picture of utter foolishness.

> *Blessed is the one*
>> *who does not walk in step with the wicked*
>> *or stand in the way that sinners take*
>> *or sit in the company of mockers,*
>> *but whose delight is in the law of the LORD,*
>> *and who meditates on his law day and night.* (vv. 1–2)

The first word mentioned in Psalm 1:1 is *blessed.* Throughout the Bible, we find two different Hebrew words for "bless" or "blessing." A *barak*[6] is a blessing based on grace; it's the most common type of blessing from God. This blessing is given without consideration to man's effort. It comes from mercy or unmerited favor. When God gives grace, He's giving a *barak* blessing. It's not earned.

The second word we find is *asre.*[7] This blessing is based on merit; it's given as a reward. It is given because you did something to earn it. You worked for it in some way. When God blesses us, sometimes it's because of His grace. But sometimes God blesses us because of a good decision we have made and because of our own actions.

One day I was at a bookstore with my eldest daughter, Kayla. She was on a lunch break from work, and I went over to spend some time with her. I needed to withdraw some money from the ATM, but it wasn't working. So we walked across the street to the bank, and I withdrew some cash. I gave twenty dollars to Kayla just because I love her. I gave her a *barak* kind of blessing.

That same evening, right before midnight, I looked out my window, and I saw Kayla tediously painting the lengthy black wrought-iron fence in our backyard. She had told my wife, Renee, a few days prior that she needed some extra cash, so Renee told her she would give her five hundred dollars if she painted the fence, which had become faded over the years. So when Kayla chose to paint the fence, her mother gave her five hundred dollars. Kayla received an *asre* kind of blessing because she did something to earn it.

Similarly, when the Israelites obeyed God by walking around the walls of Jericho for seven days—doing everything the Lord had asked them to do, exactly as He had asked them to do it—He blessed them for their obedience. God bestowed on them an *asre* blessing as a reward by giving them not only the city of Jericho but also the entire land of Canaan. Now if God had caused the city's officials to approach the Israelites in the wilderness and hand them the keys to the kingdom, it would have been the grace of God placing a gift right into the laps of His people. It would have been a *barak* blessing, since the Israelites had done nothing to earn it.

This insight changes everything about our understanding of Psalm 1 because the word *blessed* in Psalm 1:1 is not *barak*. It's not talking about God pouring unmerited favor upon our lives because

He is gracious and kind. The word the Bible uses for *blessed* in Psalm 1:1 is the word *asre*, which conveys that some blessings and rewards can be ours based on our willingness to obey.

There are two decisions we make that determine whether or not we are blessed:

1. WHAT TO AVOID?

First, there are things we need to avoid. Psalm 1 says a blessed person does not walk with the wicked, does not stand with the sinners, and does not sit with the mockers. Notice the progression of steps from walking (being on the move) to standing (coming to a complete stop) to sitting (settling in a position for a long period of time). Have you ever been in trouble because of sin? This is probably how you got there.

At the start, you were just *walking* with coworkers and friends who didn't know God. You weren't engaged in disobedience, but you listened to advice from the world. You didn't intend to participate in anything sinful. You simply were walking along and gave an ear to certain things that are contrary to God's Word.

Then you *stood*. You decided a little indulgence couldn't be that bad, so you endeavored to linger, to catch a glimpse, and to have a taste. Originally you were just walking along, but then you stood with sinners, engaging in things that were once a violation of your conscience and your beliefs.

Eventually, you *sat down* with mockers and began to laugh along with them. You were so wrapped up in sin that you began to ridicule righteousness and godliness. Your life was cast in a new mold. You became a part of the crowd that shamelessly disobeys the Word of the Lord.

What if one of the Israelite soldiers had snuck away from

the line to fraternize with the enemy? Perhaps he had decided he was just going to listen to what the Jerichoites had to say. But then he found himself lingering long enough to observe all the ungodly rituals the people of Jericho were engaging in. It looked like fun—a lot more fun than marching in a line around the walls of the city. Pretty soon, he was laughing and reveling with them, and suddenly he was on the wrong team, headed in the wrong direction.

2. WHAT TO AIM FOR?

After exposing the inevitable and unfortunate progression of foolish disobedience, Psalm 1 moves on to detail the things we need to attach ourselves to if we want to live a blessed life instead. Verse two tells us to delight ourselves in God's Word, the Bible, and to meditate on it day and night. This means you spend time reading the Word of God—not just for five minutes before you head to work or before you go to bed. You treasure the Lord's commands, and you think about them throughout the morning, afternoon, and evening. This is the key to being blessed, and it's very similar to what God said in Joshua 1:8: "Keep this Book of the Law always on your lips; meditate on it day and night, so that you may be careful to do everything written in it. Then you will be prosperous and successful."

Psalm 1:3 says that the person who cherishes the law of God "is like a tree planted by streams of water, which yields its fruit in season and whose leaf does not wither—whatever they do prospers." By taking a closer look at the imagery used in this verse, we discover that those who attach themselves to the Word of God will be blessed with strength, refreshment, and nourishment just like a well-watered tree. They will be productive in the kingdom of God and have life and longevity. Everything they do will prosper.

But those who do not honor the Lord "are like chaff that the wind blows away" (Ps. 1:4). We see this principle demonstrated unequivocally in the Battle of Jericho when God's people clearly obeyed His word. They were prosperous and blessed as a result. But on the other side of that equation, the people of Jericho were idolatrous and disobedient—and their famously fortified city was handed to the Israelites in a matter of days.

MORE THAN ENOUGH

There's an upbeat song we often sing at Shepherd Church called "One Day," by the Australian band Hillsong United. Whenever we sing it during our time of worship, the lyrics replay in my head and I find myself humming the tune for the rest of the day. The chorus talks about the abundance of God's blessings and how He is more than enough for us.

The song reminds me of a great miracle that happened when Jesus called His first disciples in Luke 5:1–11. One day on the Lake of Gennesaret, He was teaching God's Word from inside the boat to a crowd of people who were standing along the shore. The boat belonged to a fisherman named Simon, whom Jesus later would call Peter. Simon was standing nearby, washing his nets with the other fishermen.

Jesus said to Simon, "Put out into deep water, and let down the nets for a catch" (v. 4).

Simon replied, "Master, we've worked hard all night and

haven't caught anything. But because you say so, I will let down the nets" (v. 5).

Once Simon let the boat out into deeper water and lowered the nets, he and his friend caught such a large number of fish that their nets began to break. They quickly called over to their partners in the other boat to come and help them. When the other boat arrived, they filled both boats with so many fish that they began to sink. The men were greatly astonished.

Immediately, Simon fell at Jesus' knees and said, "Go away from me, Lord. I am a sinful man!" (v. 8).

Jesus said to him, "Don't be afraid; from now on you will fish for people" (v. 10). So Simon, along with James and John who were Simon's partners, pulled their boats up on shore, left everything, and followed the Lord.

There are so many poignant aspects of this story to me. First, for some unknown reason, Simon, the expert fisherman, heeded the advice of a man he hardly knew. Maybe it was the authority by which Christ gave the command. Maybe Simon had been listening to Jesus' teaching as he washed his nets, and thought, *Hey, this guy really knows what He's talking about.* Whatever the reason, we know that Simon simply obeyed, and his obedience brought about three wonderful results:

1. GREATER BLESSINGS

The men caught so many fish that the boats began to sink. Even though they had been fishing all night and caught nothing. Even though the fish were not biting. Even though Simon was the expert fisherman and knew better. They obeyed. And like the lyrics of Hillsong's "One Day," they were so blessed their nets could hardly contain it. When you obey God, He will bless you.

2. A GREATER TASK

After the large catch of fish, Jesus said to His first disciples, "Follow me, and I will make you fishers of men" (Matt. 4:19 ESV). Instead of catching fish, they were going to receive a greater calling from the Lord. They would now catch men, which means they would win souls for the kingdom of God. Instead of mending nets, they would now mend hearts.

3. GREATER FAITH

It took a small measure of faith for the disciples to cast their nets on the other side of the boat, but it led them to a place where they could take a greater step of faith and leave absolutely everything behind to follow Jesus (Luke 5:11). Oswald Chambers wrote, "The stamp of the saint is that he can waive his own rights and obey the Lord Jesus."[8] When we are faithful and obedient in the small things along our journey, God leads us to a greater level of faith and responsibility.

> WHEN WE ARE FAITHFUL AND OBEDIENT IN THE SMALL THINGS ALONG OUR JOURNEY, GOD LEADS US TO A GREATER LEVEL OF FAITH AND RESPONSIBILITY.

We become bolder for the gospel and believe in Him for greater miracles in our lives and in the lives of those for whom we are praying. Jesus said numerous times, "You of little faith." He said that if we had faith as small as a mustard seed that we could move mountains and that nothing would be impossible for us (Matt. 17:20).

Joshua and the Israelites were faithful in the seemingly small task of obeying the Lord's instructions. As a result, God gave them greater blessings as they inherited the entire land of Canaan.

He gave them a greater calling as they became a testament to the world of His matchlessness. And He gave them greater faith as they continued to trust in His goodness and promises. When we choose to obey God, the result is that our blessings, callings, and faith will be increased. We will have more than enough of what we need. And these bountiful blessings will propel us forward to victory.

STAYING THE COURSE

You may have heard the old legend about a dispute between the American navy and the Canadian authorities. Though it's largely based on myth, the story purports the following to be the actual transcript of the radio conversation a US naval ship had with Canadian authorities off the coast of Newfoundland one chilly October:

> AMERICANS: Please divert your course fifteen degrees to the north to avoid a collision.
>
> CANADIANS: Recommend you divert *your* course fifteen degrees to the south to avoid a collision.
>
> AMERICANS: This is the captain of a US Navy ship. I say again, divert *your* course.
>
> CANADIANS: No, I say again, you divert *your* course.
>
> AMERICANS: This is the aircraft carrier USS *Abraham Lincoln*, the second largest ship in the United States' Atlantic Fleet. We are accompanied by three destroyers, three cruisers, and numerous support vessels. I demand that you change your course fifteen degrees north. That's

one-five degrees north, or counter measures will be undertaken to ensure the safety of this ship.
CANADIANS: This is a lighthouse. Your call.[9]

Whatever course you may be on today, I have asked you to journey with me in a walk of faith to see the walls fall down in your personal Jericho. But after a few days, weeks, or even months have passed and you're still striving to be faithful with the steps you have learned so far, you may be wondering if you're still heading in the right direction.

Like you, it's possible that on the sixth day of their journey, the Israelites may have looked up at the colossal walls of Jericho and wondered if they were on a fool's errand. What if tomorrow, after their seventh circuit around the city and giving a shout, nothing happened and they had to walk away in total disgrace? Whenever a person is on the verge of victory or accomplishing something extraordinary, it's perfectly natural to second-guess whether all his or her time and hard work have been in vain.

Overcoming this feeling will go beyond perseverance and determination and into the region of faith and obedience. Everything in your flesh will demand that you quit, that you divert course immediately to avoid impending doom. But the difference between the naval ship and us is the fact that we've placed our trust in someone much greater than ourselves. In the story above, the captain of the aircraft carrier had placed his faith in his own ability, knowledge, and power. But ultimately, he was wrong about the ship's trajectory.

God is more powerful than all the world's naval fleets combined. His divine guidance is more reliable and accurate than the best GPS system money can buy. His Word says He will make your paths straight when you trust in Him with all your heart (Prov. 3:5–6).

After you have been cruising along slowly and steadily for a while in your journey, you may find that impatience is beginning to settle in. You may even be looking for quick solutions or fixes just because obedience seems so difficult to accomplish. But the truth is, great reward comes from obedience. It may not be easy, but it certainly will be worth it in the end. You must continue to follow the steps the Lord has instructed you to take, pushing aside that nagging sense that you should swerve onto an easier road.

When God asked the people to walk around the walls of Jericho, He didn't ask them to do something difficult. His directions were simple, though they may not have made complete sense to the Israelites. Likewise, once you sense and understand God's direction for your life, you must be obedient.

Imagine trying to discipline your child because he or she is using rude language. Every time he or she calls a person "stupid" or tells you or someone else to "shut up," you put him or her on a time-out. Most likely, the child will cry and yell and scream and throw a fit. Everything inside you will compel you to go and console your child and tell him or her that everything will be okay. You'll be tempted to make the discomfort stop by letting him or her off time-out prematurely and offering the child a lollipop.

But the best path is to follow through with the correction— no early release from the time-out and no lollipops to make it all better. Your child's character is at stake. So with patient perseverance, you hold fast until the time-out is over and have a loving talk with your child afterward to ensure he or she understands why he or she was being disciplined. Following through so that your child learns to obey the rules and respect other people is just good parenting. Eventually, he or she may even thank you for it.

It's the same in your current struggle. There may come a moment when you want to throw in the towel or speed up the process, and I'm sure there had to have been at least one Israelite soldier outside the walls of Jericho on that sixth day who felt the same way you do. But these are the defining moments that make great men and women, heroes and saints. In fact, extraordinary people look forward to the moments when resistance is strongest so that they can overcome. Embrace this stage in your journey. It's a special moment when you grit your teeth and say, "Okay. This is what separates me from everyone else who gives up when the going gets tough."

Every day—not *some* days, but *every* day of your life—decide you are going to live for the Lord. Make a decision to walk in faith—that no matter what God asks you to do, you are going to do it. No matter how silly. No matter how ridiculous. Just obey. Know that joy and victory result when you obey God's plan for your life. That may mean continuing to work on a marriage you feel like giving up on. It may mean moving in to a smaller house so you can live within your means or bless kingdom causes with your finances. It could mean that if the Lord asks you to stop worrying, you treat this command with the same sense of solemn obedience as, "Thou shalt not kill."

Perhaps it's time for you to finally begin to tithe, bring God in as a partner in all your financial decisions, "and see if [He] will not throw open the floodgates of heaven and pour out so much blessing that there will not be room enough to store it" (Mal. 3:10).

The Lord might tell you to change your career or let go of some associations that are hindering you spiritually. He may ask you to apologize to a loved one or forgive an old friend. Whatever the task—large or small, silly or significant—know that if you obey the Lord, you will set into motion the amazing plan He has for your life.

In the presence of Aryeh, Seth, Caleb, and the rest of the soldiers, Joshua approached Eliakim, whose eyes were still downcast.

"Eliakim, look at me," Joshua commanded.

The young soldier felt a pit in his stomach. Joshua had already given him a second chance just a few short days ago by saving him from certain death in the wilderness, welcoming him back to camp, and keeping his attempted desertion a secret. *Then I had to open my big, foolish mouth and probably make him regret his decision to show me mercy*, Eliakim thought.

"I can appreciate your zeal," Joshua said. "But we must be patient and simply obey God's command. There is nothing more important than this one thing."

Eliakim nodded. He was immensely relieved and amazed that Joshua would show him mercy and kindness once again. Then Joshua turned and addressed the rest of the soldiers and the priests.

"Sons of Israel, listen to me," he announced. "Go about your duties today with hope and expectancy for the blessing of the Lord. Save your courage for tomorrow, for tomorrow Jericho will be ours."

A PRAYER FOR TODAY

Heavenly Father, thank You for Your commands, which are righteous and perfect. I confess I have disobeyed You by placing my trust in worldly concepts and created things rather than in You, the Creator. Please forgive me. Help me to surrender control, fear, and any desire to fit in with the culture. I'm so glad You've shown me the way I should go in order to live a blessed life. I want to delight in Your Word and obey Your commands, for Your Word is a lamp to my feet and a light to my path (Ps. 119:105). In Jesus' name, amen.

THE PERFECT NUMBER

Get ready for a season of joy!

Joshua took a deep breath. *This is it*, he thought. *Day seven. A moment in time that will be recorded in history as a most extraordinary victory for God's people. Or it will be one in which we will be made fools in the eyes of everyone who has been watching and waiting.* After following a highly unusual plan for the past week, the Israelites would know for certain today if God had indeed told Joshua that He would deliver the famed and fortified city of Jericho into their hands.

At daybreak, the priests and the armed men arose from a sleepless night and looked to their leader. Joshua set his jaw, looking as determined as ever. Following suit, the entire Israelite army prepared in the same way they had been doing the previous six days. They laced up their sandals, took up their weapons, and silently made their way toward the giant walls that stood in defiance before them. The women and children remained in the camp, watching and praying as the men departed. Then Joshua gave the command to march.

Although they knew the number seven was considered a divine number, there was nothing supernatural or out of the ordinary about this seventh morning. All was quiet as the army and priests made their first circle around the walls. By now, they had memorized the grooves in the giant stones that composed the walls, the ironwork of the securely barred gates, and the areas where the desert plants sprouted from the cracks. They knew how many steps it would take to walk around the entire city because they had counted. They knew how long it would take because they had timed it. Nothing had changed.

Yet today's plan was different. The Israelites would not return to camp after one lap as they did on the first through the sixth day. Instead, on this seventh day, the Israelites would walk around the walls a total of seven times according to the Lord's instructions.

At first, only a dozen or so Jerichoite soldiers stood guard at the wall walk, looking down at Joshua and his men who encircled the city as they had done all week. But when the priests and soldiers made their second lap around the confines of the city, the soldiers of Jericho called their comrades up to the wall walk to witness the spectacle.

By the third circuit around the walls, word spread around the entire city that something unusual was going on outside their gates. One short week ago, the Jerichoites were terrified about the arrival of Joshua and his men because they had heard how the God of the Israelites had set them free from captivity in Egypt, performed many miracles, and given His people victory over formidable armies like the Amorites. Now they were looking down in disbelief at the foreigners who simply were marching around the walls of their city. What kind of military strategy was this?

"Don't they have anything better to do?" one of the Jerichoite soldiers mocked.

"What a comedy show this is!" another laughed.

"Perhaps all that walking in circles has made them dizzy!" still another teased.

Ignoring their taunts, the Israelites made their fourth lap, and then their fifth. All their years of training, waiting, and walking had led up to this very moment in time. Instead of becoming wearier with each circuit, the army's anticipation grew stronger as they imagined storming the famed city once the walls came crashing down supernaturally. By the start of the Israelites' sixth trip around the walls, the Jerichoite men grew tired of watching the strangers march monotonously. They ran out of jokes and eventually went back to their business.

The sun had just reached the midmorning hour as Joshua, the priests, and the soldiers approached their seventh circle around Jericho. Each person became more and more certain that they were about to participate in something truly extraordinary. Their hearts raced. Perspiration fell from their brows. The priests blew their trumpets unceasingly.[1] The soldiers' hands clutched their swords. Their eyes darted back and forth from the marching line to the wall, waiting for Joshua's signal. It could be any moment now.

Every single one of them had been transformed by the past week's events. Joshua marched with confident trust in the greatness of God as he led the people around walls that now seemed miniscule compared to the size of their Lord. Caleb, ever bold and loyal, walked alongside his friend Joshua, ready to fight a battle that would make their victory over the Amalekites look like child's play. On the other side of the wall, Rahab and her family waited faithfully for God's plan to culminate, knowing that their deliverance—and a new beginning—would come speedily.

With each step Aryeh took, he realized that strategy and might are not nearly as important as holiness in securing victory from the Lord. Instead of running away or isolating himself out of fear, Eliakim courageously marched shoulder to shoulder with his brethren. Seth walked with purpose, for all his years of wandering had finally ceased, and all his consistency had finally paid off; now he would fight for what the Lord had promised his generation. And the entire army knew that obedience would bring God's blessing in His perfect timing.

That time was now. Once the entire Israelite company went around the walls of Jericho for the seventh time, the priests sounded a long blast on the trumpets. Then Joshua raised his voice and commanded the army, "Shout! For the LORD has given you the city! The city and all that is in it are to be devoted to the LORD. Only Rahab the prostitute and all who are with her in her house shall be spared, because she hid the spies we sent."[2]

The entire army shouted, their roar joining the trumpet blast. Not even a split second passed to allow any of them to hold his breath or pause in anticipation of what was to come. Instantly, the walls collapsed before them—just as God had promised. Huge stones fell from their places, piled on top of one another in a heap, and shook the ground upon impact. Without waiting for the earth to stop quivering, Joshua and the Israelites ran up the hill. They climbed over the giant bricks with adrenaline surging through their veins, charged straight through the dismantled gates, and took the city on that glorious seventh day.

The number seven is said to be the number of perfection. It is the Lord's number and signifies sacred completeness.[3] The number seven appears 457 times in the New International Version of the Bible, occurring first in Genesis 2:2–3 when God finished creating the world on the seventh day and rested.[4] He then blessed the seventh day and made it holy.

The Lord gave Abraham a sevenfold blessing in Genesis 12:2–3. There are seven parables in Matthew 13 and seven miracles listed in the gospel of John. Jesus told us to forgive a brother or a sister who has sinned against us "up to seventy times seven" in Matthew 18:22 (NKJV). And the book of Revelation—the last book of the Bible—is rife with this significant number: there are seven churches, seven spirits of God, seven golden lampstands, seven stars, seven angels, seven seals of judgment, the Lamb with seven horns and seven eyes, seven trumpets, seven thunders, a red dragon with seven heads, seven plagues, seven bowls of God's wrath, seven hills, and seven kings. That's a lot of sevens!

Not only is seven a cardinal number in the Bible but it is also the central number to our story. God asked Joshua and the Israelites to march around the wall of Jericho for seven days led by seven priests. On the seventh day, they had to march around the wall seven times. It was not a random number. It was a number of purpose.

Seven was the Lord's number for the Lord's people to bring about the victory they desperately needed. It was the key that unlocked the door to the promised land—to bury the past after four hundred years of slavery and forty years of wandering in a desert. It ushered in an amazing season of joy for the Israelites as they took hold of blessings the Lord had been patiently waiting to bestow on them.

When God said in Joshua 6:2, "See, I have delivered Jericho into your hands, along with its king and its fighting men," it was a bona fide guarantee to His people that He was about to bless them and give them victory. At this point in your journey around the seemingly impossible walls in your life, you still might be asking, "Is there a possibility that I will never have victory?" And the answer to that question is, absolutely not! You will have victory! I believe it is a guarantee for you, just as it was for Joshua and the Israelites, because of the magnificent promises we find throughout God's Word.

Deuteronomy 20:4 tells us that God is the one who goes with His people to fight for them and give them victory. I love how Psalm 149:4 says, "For the LORD takes delight in his people; he crowns the humble with victory." First Corinthians 15:57 makes this joyous declaration: "But thanks be to God! He gives us the victory through our Lord Jesus Christ." And 1 John 5:4–5 gives believers the assurance that "everyone born of God overcomes the world. This is the victory that has overcome the world, even our faith. Who is it that overcomes the world? Only the one who believes that Jesus is the Son of God."

Since our victories are guaranteed, the question really is not, "Will I ever have victory?" but, "How do I live in victory today?" In this seventh chapter of our journey, it's only fitting that we explore seven ways you can walk daily in the triumph the Lord your God desires for you.

1. REALIZE GOD HAS A PERFECT NUMBER FOR YOU.

Seven is the number that God gave to the Israelites in this particular battle, but I believe God has a specific number—a specific time frame—for you and every believer. In these final moments of our journey around Jericho, it's important to understand that embracing God's perfect number for you is a necessary final step to victory. Your battle could last seven days just like the Battle of Jericho, or it could be seven weeks, seven months, or seven years. It could possibly last seventy years.

Several years ago, I met a former middleweight boxer who had been deaf his entire life. He was in his seventies when I met him, and he had just had a breakthrough surgery that enabled him to hear. He showed me the small area on his skull where the special device had been implanted.

> SEVEN IS THE NUMBER THAT GOD GAVE TO THE ISRAELITES IN THIS PARTICULAR BATTLE, BUT I BELIEVE GOD HAS A SPECIFIC NUMBER—A SPECIFIC TIME FRAME—FOR YOU AND EVERY BELIEVER.

This man had been deaf for seven decades, but through modern technology he finally received the miraculous gift of hearing.

Ecclesiastes 3:1 reveals, "There is a time for everything, and a season for every activity under the heavens." Today, you may be in the season of trial and testing. But it's inevitable that a few short days, months, or years will make way for a season of joy and victory. Don't give up hope. Your triumph over the towering walls in your life is coming in God's perfect timing.

The Bible says that God has had your number of days and your number of steps written down before one of them ever came to be—before you were even born (Ps. 139:16). Isn't there tremendous comfort in knowing that the Lord is aware of your present struggle and that He knows how many steps you will need to take before victory comes? He's there with you. He knew, before you were created, that you were going to be in this situation. He knows your journey. God knows the precise number of steps and days required for your walls to come tumbling down.

Let's suppose you're a soldier walking around the fortress of Jericho next to another soldier who is 15 percent taller than you. Let's say he's a cool, six feet, five inches tall. That soldier is going to take 15 percent fewer steps than you because his legs are 15 percent longer than yours. So at the end of one lap around the walls of Jericho, you may have taken 5,000 steps, but the taller guy with the longer stride took 4,250 steps. My point is this: God knew the exact number of steps every soldier was going to take—including the number of times they would stumble on a patch of uneven ground or stop to take a drink of water. In the same way, God knows the number of your steps around the walls of your personal Jericho.

This truth reminds me of an interesting passage we find in Exodus 13 when Moses and the Israelites escaped from Egypt:

> God did not lead them on the road through the Philistine country, *though that was shorter.* For God said, "If they face war, they might change their minds and return to Egypt." So God led

the people around by the desert road toward the Red Sea. (vv. 17–18, emphasis added)

This eye-opening excerpt shows us there were a number of steps and a number of travel days that would have been easier and shorter for the Israelites. It would have gotten them to their destination more directly, but it wasn't the number God had in mind for them. The most expeditious route wouldn't have been what was best for them. The Lord knew that if His people faced opposition so quickly after escaping the Egyptians, they would have second thoughts about leaving. He knew that fear would have driven them right back into captivity. So instead, God led the Israelites by a longer route—a different number of steps and a different number of travel days—guiding them with a pillar of cloud by day and a pillar of fire by night.

This story sends a fascinating message to you and me today. God has a specific number in mind for us, and that number is perfect for many reasons. The length of your battle should in no way lead you to believe that God

> THE LENGTH OF YOUR BATTLE OR YOUR JOURNEY SHOULD IN NO WAY LEAD YOU TO BELIEVE THAT GOD HAS FORGOTTEN ABOUT YOU OR THAT THERE HAS BEEN A GLITCH IN THE GPS.

has forgotten about you or that there has been a glitch in the GPS. Your heavenly Father is privy to certain knowledge and insight you do not possess. He may be taking you on a longer route that is better and safer for you, one that grows your faith and gives you an opportunity to learn valuable lessons. Whatever your number is, know that every step of the way God is leading and guiding you to a season of victory.

2. KNOW THAT YOUR DEFINITION OF VICTORY MAY BE DIFFERENT FROM GOD'S DEFINITION.

In the midst of your journey, it's important to keep in mind that victory from your perspective and victory from God's perspective could be two different things. Your idea of victory might mean the end of pain and struggle. That might be all you care about right now. Yet the Lord's idea of victory could look entirely different. Take the cross, for example. Christ's crucifixion wasn't pain free. Do you think that was an easy thing for God or Jesus to go through? And yet the Bible says, "For the joy set before him he *endured* the cross, scorning its shame, and sat down at the right hand of the throne of God" (Heb. 12:2, emphasis added). This was the ultimate victory. Even though Jesus' journey was marked with a great deal of pain and suffering, He was victorious as He conquered sin and death and was exalted to the right hand of the Father.

God's plan for the Israelites from the beginning was to bless them and bring them to a land flowing with milk and honey. But because of their sins and disobedience, hundreds of years passed between the initial promise the Lord made to Abraham and the Israelites actually entering and taking possession of Canaan under Joshua's leadership. Despite human setbacks and errors, God's plan still stood, and victory for His people was achieved.

As we learned in days 3 and 6 of this journey, it's possible that a big part of God's plan was to cultivate holiness and obedience in His people throughout this protracted length of time. It could be that part of His plan was to allow the sins of the Israelites to demonstrate the need for the law, so that the law would demonstrate the need for God's grace that is only made available through the death, burial, and resurrection of Jesus Christ. Our heavenly Father always has a higher purpose and a perfect plan for victory that we may not always be able to see right away.

In 2 Corinthians 12:7–10, we discover that the apostle Paul endured some kind of affliction or trial he described as "a thorn in my flesh, a messenger of Satan" (v. 7). We don't know what this strange ailment was, but Paul said it was sent to him to torment him and keep him from becoming conceited. He wrote that he pleaded with God three times to take it away from him, but God said to him, "My grace is sufficient for you, for my power is made perfect in weakness" (v. 9). Basically, the Lord's answer was no, so Paul made an attitude adjustment. He wrote:

> Therefore I will boast all the more gladly about my weaknesses, so that Christ's power may rest on me. That is why, for Christ's sake, I delight in weaknesses, in insults, in hardships, in persecutions, in difficulties. For when I am weak, then I am strong. (2 Cor. 12:9–10)

Paul was a zealous man of God who performed many awesome miracles in the name of Jesus and wrote more than half of the New Testament, but these verses in 2 Corinthians tell us that there were still a few issues in his life that the Lord did not give him relief from—until the day Paul went to be with Him in heaven. By enduring these trials, Paul realized he needed the grace and power of God, and that in his weaknesses, God was glorified. In that respect, he was victorious because He succeeded at the most important reason believers are put on this earth: to bring God glory so that others might believe.

In His wisdom and sovereignty, the Lord may have a different perspective about the obstacle you're facing right now. There is a chance that you are asking God to remove it, and He may say no because your ultimate victory is going to come in heaven. And in the meantime, you will walk in victory today by relying on God's grace and His strength and by glorifying Him so that others might believe.

3. TREASURE THE LEARNING PROCESS.

Is there anything purer and more joyous than Christmas morning through the eyes of a small child? Do you remember what that was like? To be in your pajamas and wake up earlier than your parents and the rest of creation, tiptoe over to a grand and glorious Christmas tree, and behold a pile of presents nestled beneath the branches. You recognize your name written on the shiny wrapping of one of the gifts, and you pick up the box. What could it be?

Soon the rest of your family enters the room sleepily, and your mom or dad gives you the nod that means it's okay to open your present. You eagerly tear open the wrapping paper and find that it had been concealing the very thing you wanted. The fast racecar or the new doll or the video game everyone has been talking about. For a child, the best part of Christmas morning is the surprise.

But as you get older, you want the surprise much sooner. You start looking for presents in every closet in the house in the days leading up to Christmas. And when you finally find one and extract it from its hiding nook, you shake the gift to determine its weight. Maybe you feel around the package or tear the wrapping carefully to peek at what's inside. But once you've done that, the surprise is lost. Christmas morning loses a bit of joy when you know exactly what you're getting.

Buried within your current struggle or trial are seeds of truth that, when fully sprouted, are God's gift to you. It might be the precious necessity of learning patience or perseverance; it might be victory or some type of reward, be it spiritual or physical. Don't attempt to receive the gift He has for you before it's your time to receive it. Simply be obedient today, trust the Lord, and wait patiently to open the gift until He gives you that nod that lets you know the time is right. In doing so, you will not only please your Father in heaven, but also learn the lesson God wants you to learn—and this is part of the gift.

God had a special gift in store for His people at the Battle of Jericho. It was wrapped in seemingly unbreakable walls and iron gates. And like a Russian nesting doll, it contained more gifts, larger gifts—riches, abundance of land and agriculture, and a gateway to other cities that would be theirs for the taking. But the Israelites had to be patient and obey God's instructions to a tee before any of these blessings would be realized.

Joshua conveyed God's command to the army by saying in Joshua 6:10, "Do not give a war cry, do not raise your voices, do not say a word *until the day I tell you* to shout. Then shout!" (emphasis added).

The word *until* is important in the English language. It denotes our need to wait, and to submit to the leading and timing of someone or something else. From the time of our youth, we have learned that we cannot get dessert *until* we eat our dinners, and that we can't go out and play *until* our rooms are clean or we finish our homework. We start a career knowing that we won't get a paycheck *until* we complete two weeks of work. A woman doesn't give birth *until* she has carried her baby for about nine months.

In the Battle of Jericho, the Israelites had to do exactly as God said and wait until the time was right. So do we. We cannot open God's gift a second sooner. Like Joshua and the Israelites, we first have to submit to God's leading and timing, and then we can learn what He is attempting to teach us. We can either do things our own way—which seems easy but is actually the hard way—or we can do things God's way, which seems hard but is actually the easy way. There is no better plan than the one our heavenly Father has established. There is no better lesson than the one He desires to teach us. And the men and women who are patient, obedient, trusting, and eager to learn are the people who get the privilege of experiencing extraordinary triumph in their lives.

> THERE IS NO BETTER PLAN THAN THE ONE OUR HEAVENLY FATHER HAS ESTABLISHED. THERE IS NO BETTER LESSON THAN THE ONE HE DESIRES TO TEACH US.

Did you know that Laura Ingalls Wilder, the renowned author of the *Little House on the Prairie* books, was unpublished as an author of books until she was sixty-five years old? Talk about waiting a long time to achieve success by the world's standards! And yet, here's the interesting thing: even though it took her a long time to realize her dream of being an author, her works have already lasted long after she passed away in 1957.[5]

Ronald Reagan was a month shy of his seventieth birthday when he realized his dream of becoming president of the United States.[6] To date, he is the oldest man elected to the office of the president. David Seidler, who wrote the script for the 2010 Academy Award–winning film *The King's Speech*, based on the inspiring true story of King George VI, struggled in Hollywood for thirty-three years. At the age of seventy-three, he won an

Academy Award for best original screenplay.[7] Abraham was one hundred years old and his wife, Sarah, was ninety years old when the Lord fulfilled His promise to give them a child of their own, from whom a great nation would grow (Gen. 21:1–7). And Moses was eighty years old when God called him to lead the Israelites out of Egypt (Ex. 7:7).

I'm sure that the men and women in each of these extraordinary examples learned something important and valuable during the long waiting period that would prepare him or her for a season of victory. It's the same for you and me. We ought to have the attitude of Moses when he made this humble request to the Lord: "Teach me your ways so I may know you and continue to find favor with you" (Ex. 33:13). Treasure the learning process.

4. PAY YOUR COMFORT FORWARD.

There are a multitude of facets, reasons, and intricacies to the Lord's plan that we might never understand fully. But one possibility in your present situation is that God wants to use your experience to help someone else who is going through the same struggle later on down the road. In other words, you could be battling this obstacle in your life right now because, in the ultimate scheme of things, God needs you to be His hands and feet and heart to comfort someone else.

There is no comfort like the kind that comes from someone who has been through the same struggle as you have. Perhaps you have already experienced this encouragement from another person. One day, it will be time for you to pay it forward. You may not understand that right now, but I believe you're going to find yourself saying in the near or distant future, "Oh, *that's* why I went through that—so I could help this person!"

Sitting in a bustling airport a couple of weeks ago, I was feeling a bit frustrated because the flight I was supposed to take was late arriving to my gate. This delay meant I was going to miss my connecting flight home. I longed to see my wife and children, and I knew I had a full work schedule awaiting me the next day. But despite my disappointment with this unforeseen inconvenience, the events of that day in the airport quickly changed my entire perspective.

In the busy waiting area packed with travelers who were as eager to get to their next destinations as I was, I struck up a conversation with another gentleman. We were commiserating about flight delays and sharing what we did for a living, when all of a sudden, a rather effervescent and gregarious blonde woman came and sat down in the chair between us. She initiated a joyful conversation with the man I had been talking to. I deduced that they were longtime friends who hadn't seen each other in a while. In a nanosecond, this woman changed the whole tone of our conversation, which had been, "We will never get out of this terminal." Her bubbly personality and infectious joy lit up the atmosphere like an airport runway at night.

Her name was Regina, and when I asked her what she did for a living, she replied with a warm smile, "I work for the military. I help widows and families who have lost loved ones. Right now, I'm helping over four hundred individuals and families."

I sat stunned. There I was, feeling sorry for myself for missing a connecting flight home, and this woman who helps families and widows who have been devastated by war had a much better attitude than I had. After a few seconds of reflection, I said to Regina, "You must really excel at your job."

How she responded next was even more amazing. She said,

"I do! But it's not because of me. It's because of what I've been through. You see, I myself am a widow. My husband died during his military service."

Immediately, I thought about the passage of scripture that says our compassionate Lord "comforts us in all our troubles, so that we can comfort those in any trouble with the comfort we ourselves receive from God" (2 Cor. 1:3–4). I asked Regina if she had ever read these verses before, and she said "No," so I opened my Bible and read them to her.

Regina's cheerfulness and enthusiasm went up another notch as she expressed how thankful and overjoyed she was that I had shared this scripture with her. She said, "That's *exactly* who I am and what God's done in my life!"

When you view these verses in 2 Corinthians in light of the trials you're facing, you learn that the main reason God gives us comfort—which you so desperately want right now—is so that you might give comfort to others. God wants you to have a heart that is full of compassion, like His. So there's a high probability that God has planned for you to help others who are struggling in the future.

5. SEE THE GLIMMERS OF HOPE.

My wife, Renee, and I were talking recently about the people we know who are enduring difficult seasons of trials and suffering. Many of our church members are fighting difficult illnesses or dealing with tragic losses. There's a two-year-old little girl from our church who choked on a popcorn kernel, stopped breathing, and is now in a coma. Our hearts are burdened for so many married couples who are on the brink of divorce, barely holding on by a thread. We know parents who are praying fervently for high school or college-aged children who seem to have lost their way.

Reflecting on these great challenges, Renee said to me with tears collecting in her eyes, "You know, God is so gracious to give us little signs along the way that provide glimmers of hope. He will send us some kind of sign that enables us to get through the most difficult storm, but oftentimes we fail to see the sign if we're not looking for it."

GOD IS SO GRACIOUS TO GIVE US LITTLE SIGNS ALONG THE WAY THAT PROVIDE GLIMMERS OF HOPE.

How true that is! As you wait for your season of victory, it's easy to get focused on the negative and the seeming impossibility of what you are facing. But if you look—if you lift your eyes and look around—the Lord is so faithful to sprinkle glimmers of hope here and there to encourage you to keep trusting and pressing on.

Louis Zamperini was a lieutenant in World War II whose plane crashed eight hundred miles south of Hawaii in the middle of the Pacific Ocean in 1943. Perched on a raft with only two other survivors of the eleven people who had been on the doomed B-24, Louis was pushed to the limits of his will and resolve. He and his companions fought off sharks, survived thirst and starvation, and miraculously remained unscathed after enduring forty-five minutes of machine-gun fire by a Japanese bomber.

As they drifted for thousands of miles with no rescue in sight, God gave them tiny glimmers of hope. They found a few chocolate bars in the pockets of the raft. Merciful rain showers poured down water for them to drink when their bodies had become gaunt from near-fatal dehydration. Once, an albatross landed on Louis's head, and he reached up slowly and caught it. The men feasted on the seabird like kings and then used its bones to fashion claws to catch the occasional fish that swam just beneath the surface of the water.[8] Seeing the stars strewn across the night sky reminded Louis that God was still there. "When you reach the end of your rope and there's nowhere else to turn . . . you're going to look up," Louis said later.[9]

Each of these small and sporadic instances served as a glimmer of hope that, somehow, the men might get through this situation alive.

After thirty-three days at sea, crew member Francis McNamara died. On day forty-seven, Louis Zamperini and fellow survivor Russell Allen Phillips were picked up by Japanese sailors. They were held in prison camps for more than two years where they were tortured viciously, injected with strange substances, and deprived of food. Somehow, the defiant American with an unbreakable spirit survived. When the Japanese surrendered and the war ended in 1945, Louis was released.

Back home in America, he received the Purple Heart and many other honors, but he suffered from post-traumatic stress disorder, including haunting nightmares from his horrific experiences in Japan. He drank heavily to cope, and his marriage was on the rocks. At the prompting of his wife, Louis attended a crusade in Los Angeles in 1949 where a young evangelist named Billy Graham shared the gospel.[10] During the invitation, Louis remembered a prayer he had spoken on that little raft in the middle of the Pacific Ocean six years earlier, promising God, "If you save me, I will serve you forever."[11]

Louis stepped forward and gave his life to Christ. He forgave his captors and went on to become an inspirational speaker. His incredible story is told in the book *Unbroken* by Laura Hillenbrand, who is the best-selling author of *Seabiscuit*. Like Louis Zamperini, when you are going through the worst storm of your life—even when you are in the midst of a terribly hopeless situation—if you'll look for them, you'll see the glimmers of hope from the Lord.

In Luke 1:5–25, we meet a man named Zechariah who was a priest in Israel. He and his wife, Elizabeth, were very old and observed all God's commands blamelessly. Although they had prayed diligently for a child for many years, they were not able to conceive. One day, after Zechariah was chosen to go into the temple of God to burn incense, the angel Gabriel appeared to him, standing at the right side of the altar of incense. Zechariah was so terrified by the sight of the angel of the Lord that he trembled in fear. Gabriel told Zechariah not to be afraid, and explained in detail that he and his wife would have a son named John, and that this child would be the forerunner to Christ.

Zechariah then asked Gabriel for a sign. "How can I be sure of this?" he said. "I am an old man and my wife is well along in years" (v. 18).

Time out for a minute. I understand that Zechariah had a hard time believing he would have a son in his old age and that his son would prepare the way for the Messiah. But right in front of him stood Gabriel, a celestial being! He experienced something supernatural that very few people have ever experienced. Gabriel told Zechariah this fantastic news, and the old man asked for a sign. Gabriel probably thought to himself, *What am I, chopped liver? You want a sign? I'll give you a sign!* So he told Zechariah he wouldn't be able to speak until the baby was born, and that's exactly what happened. Zechariah wasn't able to say a word until his son John—who later became known as John the Baptist—was born.

When you're in the middle of a storm, you've got to look for those signs. Instead of getting bogged down by how impossible your situation may be or how improbable victory may seem, look up. You may not see an angel standing in front of you as Zechariah did, but God wants to show you a glimmer of hope. Open your eyes and look around and you will see it.

Perhaps your glimmer of hope was simply seeing the title of this book, *Walls Fall Down*, and knowing somehow it was just the message you needed to hear. Something you've read along the course of this journey may have served as a sign to buoy you in the middle of a sea of turmoil, giving you hope that you will get through it. Maybe you looked up at the stars of the sky or witnessed the miracle of a baby being born and realized that God has a plan for you. These glimmers of hope are there to remind you that God hasn't forgotten about you. He sees you! Your season of victory is coming. Just keep your eyes on the horizon and a prayer ever upon your lips.

6. ADOPT AN ATTITUDE OF PRAISE.

Praise and rejoicing were part of God's curious plan for Joshua and the Israelites to defeat the city of Jericho. On the seventh day, He instructed the priests to sound the trumpet blast and the soldiers to hoot and holler like a bunch of hillbillies at a hoedown. Then Joshua commanded the army, "Shout! For the LORD has given you the city!" (Josh. 6:16). Their praise was part of the plan and it resulted in victory. Likewise, you should celebrate and praise God right now in the midst of your personal Jericho because He has already given you the victory.

God said in Isaiah 43:21, "The people I formed for myself that they may proclaim my praise." This means that you and I were made to praise the Lord. This is especially important in your present struggle because praise was the final weapon God used to bring down the walls of Jericho and usher the Israelites in to their season of blessing.

So what exactly is praise? It's an exclusive honor that should be given only to God. In praising Him, we are engaging in enthusiastic exaltation just as a zealous fan who wears his or her team's colors and shouts adulation from the stands at a football game. And despite the praise given to athletes, sports teams, actors, singers, rock bands, and politicians, no one is worthy of our praise except the Lord God Almighty. Praise is a joyful surrender to His sovereignty.

> PRAISE WAS THE FINAL WEAPON GOD USED TO BRING DOWN THE WALLS OF JERICHO AND USHER THE ISRAELITES IN TO THEIR SEASON OF BLESSING.

We praise God for who He is and what He does. He is Creator, sovereign, omnipresent, omniscient, and omnipotent. He is full of grace, mercy, and love. There is no one like Him in heaven or on earth. He provides for us; He protects, promises, pursues, purifies, and perfects. Our praise reminds us of His unfailing character. Psalm 150 says that "everything that has breath" should praise God for His mighty acts of power and for the Lord's surpassing greatness. It instructs us to praise Him with every instrument known to man.

You may not think of praise as a weapon or an effective tool, but it is. Ephesians 6:12 reveals that our battle is not physical but spiritual, and 2 Corinthians 10:3–5 tells us that the effective weapons we need to use in this warfare should not be mere human weapons but godly weapons, which are mighty and powerful.

Praise was essential in the victory King Jehoshaphat and the army of Judah had over the armies of Ammon, Moab, and Mount Seir in 2 Chronicles 20:20–23. Going out into the wilderness of Tekoa, the Bible says, "the king appointed singers to walk ahead of the army, singing to the LORD and praising him for his holy splendor. This is what they sang: 'Give thanks to the LORD; his faithful love endures forever!'" (v. 21 NLT). What happened next is quite astonishing. When the people began to sing and give praise, God caused their enemies to start fighting among themselves even though they were allies. The armies of Ammon, Moab, and Mount Seir attacked and destroyed one another.

What are you battling today? Discouragement, disappointment, depression, or disease? Perhaps you are fighting fear, guilt, or low self-esteem? Maybe you feel as though you are losing a war against forces that are attacking your marriage, your family, or your finances? Though your battle may appear to be physical, you are actually engaged in a spiritual battle. Left alone to fight with human weapons (your intellect, strength, and resources), there is no doubt you will be defeated. But Romans 8:31–37 makes it clear that when God is for us, no one can be against us, and with His help, we are more than conquerors.

In a sense, praise is verbalizing our faith in the Lord's strength and victory in our lives. Praise is powerful because it prepares our hearts and ushers us in to the presence of God, as Psalm 100:4 instructs, "Enter his gates with thanksgiving and his courts with praise; give thanks to him and praise his name." As you lift your hands toward heaven and praise God from the center of your heart, He will show up and fight your battles for you just as He did for Joshua and the Israelites at Jericho, as well as for Jehoshaphat, Gideon, and countless others. Praise sets the stage for a miracle.

George Müller was a nineteenth-century Christian evangelist and the director of an orphanage in Bristol, England, caring for more than ten thousand orphans during his lifetime.[12] Müller was a man of great faith and prayer. He never made requests of others for financial support and never went into debt. God always provided for the needs of the orphanage. On one well-documented occasion, the housemother of the orphanage informed Müller that the children were dressed and ready for school but there was no food for them to eat. Müller instructed her to take the three hundred children into the dining room and have them sit at the tables. He praised God and thanked God for the food even though the tables were bare. Within minutes, a baker knocked on the door.

"Mr. Müller, last night I couldn't sleep," the baker said. "Somehow I knew that you would need bread this morning. I got up and baked three batches for you."

The baker brought in the bread, and soon there was another knock at the door. It was the milkman. His cart had broken down in front of the orphanage. Knowing the milk would spoil by the time the wheel was fixed, the milkman asked George if he could use some free milk. George smiled as the milkman brought in ten large cans of milk. It was just enough for the children.[13]

Before George Müller ever knew there was a problem, God was already preparing the solution. Then, once Müller was made aware of their predicament, He praised the Lord, which escorted God's provision into the orphanage. When all the doors seem closed and there's no victory in sight, praise the Lord in the hallway until He opens a door.

We see this principle at work in Acts 16:16–36 when Paul and Silas were wrongfully beaten and imprisoned in Philippi. At midnight, they prayed and sang hymns to God as the other prisoners listened. Suddenly, an earthquake shook the prison violently, causing the doors to fly open and all the prisoners' chains to come loose. When the jailer woke up and saw the prison doors open, he was about to kill himself because he thought the prisoners had escaped. But Paul shouted, "Don't harm yourself! We are all here!" (v. 28).

The Philippian jailer called for lights, and seeing Paul and Silas, he fell trembling before them and asked, "Sirs, what must I do to be saved?" (v. 30).

They replied, "Believe in the Lord Jesus, and you will be saved—you and your household" (v. 31). At that hour, the jailer and his entire household believed and were baptized. In the morning, the jailer received an order from the magistrates to release Paul and Silas.

Despite their harsh and unjust circumstances, and in the darkest hour of the night, Paul and Silas chose to praise the Lord. And how did God respond? He showed up in a profound way, setting them free and using them to save the souls of a jailer and his family. Like these men of faith, you and I must adopt an attitude of praise. Praise the Lord whenever you are caught between a rock and a hard place. Praise Him whenever the journey appears to be taking too long. Praise God whenever your path seems to lead you on an unwanted detour. Keep on praising Him, knowing that power is unleashed in praise. It's only a matter of time before the Lord shows up and delivers you in a mighty way (Ps. 50:15).

7. PREPARE TO HEAR THE TRUMPET SOUND.

As we return to the final verses of our story in Joshua chapter 6, we learn in verse 20 that when the priests sounded the trumpets, and the entire army shouted after their seventh circuit around the city of Jericho on the seventh day, the walls collapsed. We see the significance of the trumpet sound come into play many years later in 2 Chronicles 13 during an intriguing battle between Jeroboam, the king of Israel, and Abijah, the king of Judah. In those days, the nation of Israel was split into two kingdoms—Israel and Judah—both of which had a long succession of good and bad kings. In this particular instance, Jeroboam was the bad king and Abijah was the good king.

One day, these two kings went to battle against each other, and the Bible says that Abijah had a force of four hundred thousand fighting men, while Jeroboam had double that amount with eight hundred thousand soldiers. Despite being terribly outnumbered, Abijah stood on a mountain and declared to Jeroboam and his men:

> As for us, the LORD is our God, and we have not forsaken him . . .
> But you have forsaken him. God is with us; he is our leader. His
> priests with their trumpets will sound the battle cry against you.
> Men of Israel, do not fight against the LORD, the God of your
> father, for you will not succeed. (2 Chron. 13:10–12)

Meanwhile, Jeroboam, the crafty fellow, sent a rear ambush behind Abijah and his troops. But when the men of Judah turned and saw they were being attacked from both sides, they cried out to the Lord, blew their trumpets, and raised the battle cry. The Bible says, "At the sound of their battle cry, God routed Jeroboam and all Israel before Abijah and Judah. The Israelites fled before Judah, and God delivered them into their hands" (vv. 15–16). It sounds to me as though the Lord responded to the trumpet sound and the cry of His people. In fact, verse 18 reveals that "the people of Judah were victorious because they relied on the LORD, the God of their ancestors."

All this pictures a future battle and a future era when another trumpet is going to sound. At the end of the world, the culmination of all things, the Bible says God will send His angels with a loud trumpet call and gather together believers in Christ—those who are resting in their graves and those who are still alive.[14] This, my friend, is the ultimate victory. It's triumph over earthly struggles; it's the final defeat over all that ails us.

The blessed return of Jesus will be a reality. Those who have placed their faith in His saving death, burial, and resurrection will be taken up to heaven to be with the Lord forever. That's the trumpet sound I'm looking forward to!

Dear friend, in your own epic journey, I hope you will always remember that the promised trumpet sound of your personal triumph is a few simple steps away, just as it was for Joshua and the Israelites at the Battle of Jericho. It might take seven days or seven years, but that trumpet *will* sound. Wait for it. Listen for it. That jubilant melody will announce triumph as your walls fall down and pave the way for you to take hold of the blessings God has in store for you. In the meantime, like the hero of any great story, take what you have learned and apply it to your daily life:

1. Stand in awe of the greatness of God, knowing that your problems instantly shrink in the magnitude of His power and sovereignty.
2. Place your trust in God's unique plan for your life, having faith that His plan is perfect and surer than the rising sun.
3. Make your struggle a holy exercise by putting God first in your life and endeavoring to honor Him in all that you do—even in the simple and mundane.
4. Immerse yourself in a culture of like-minded people, realizing that no battle is won alone and that there is power in banding together with others who are striving to adopt the mind of Christ.

5. Be consistent in your Christian walk, trusting that the Lord is working behind the scenes to lead you toward victory with each faithful step you take.

6. Obey God's commands not only out of your love for Him, but also because you understand there is a direct correlation between your obedience and His blessing on your life.

7. Embrace the fact that just as seven is a divine and perfect number, God has a perfect number for you regarding your current trial—and that a season of joy and victory is coming.

Stored together in your artillery, accessed and utilized properly, the seven principles you've learned will cause the very foundation of the walls that stand before you to tremble as you anticipate God bringing about complete and total victory.

⟜

Like a mighty firestorm, the Israelites swept through Jericho, devoting the city to the Lord and destroying with the sword everything in it as He had commanded them to do. Joshua said to the two young men who had spied out the land, "Go into the prostitute's house and bring her out and all who belong to her, in accordance with your oath to her."[15] So the men ran to Rahab's home and brought her out along with her father and mother, her brothers and sisters, and all who belonged to her. They set Rahab and her family outside of the camp of Israel where they lived safely for the rest of their days.

Then, the Israelites made their conquest complete by

burning the entire city and everything in it. Joshua, Caleb, Aryeh, Seth, Eliakim, and the rest of God's people stood in awe of the total and irreversible victory Yahweh had given to them. They put the silver and gold and the articles of bronze and iron into the treasury of the Lord's house. "So the Lord was with Joshua, and his fame spread throughout the land."[16]

Joshua was a faithful man and a righteous leader of Israel all his days. He led the Israelites through many great battles, because the conquest of Canaan did not end with Jericho. Jericho was just the beginning. It was the gateway to the promised land. The vast territory God had promised to His people stretched as far north as Sidon, bordering the land of the Hittites, and as far south as Kadesh. It hugged the Mediterranean Sea on the west and stretched past the Dead Sea to the edge of the land of the Moabites and Ammonites.

After the fall of Jericho, Joshua took thirty thousand of his best fighting men and attacked Ai in the night. God delivered the king of Ai, his people, his city, and his land to the hands of the Israelites. Next, when the five kings of the Amorites joined forces to attack Gibeon, Israel's ally, Joshua and his men marched all night from Gilgal and took them by surprise. Yahweh threw the armies of the Amorites into confusion before Israel, so Joshua and the Israelites defeated them completely at Gibeon (Josh. 10:1–11).

Then Joshua and the Israelites went out and took all the southern cities in one campaign as the Lord God of Israel fought for them. According to His command, they subdued the entire region, which included the hill country, the Negev, the western foothills, and the mountain slopes. They left no survivors.

Next, they went up to fight against the northern kingdoms. The Lord said to Joshua, "Do not be afraid of them, because by this time tomorrow I will hand all of them over to Israel" (Josh. 11:16). So Joshua took the entire land, just as Yahweh had directed Moses, and he gave it as an inheritance to Israel according to their tribal divisions (vv. 7–23). He and the rest of God's people conquered the unconquerable, and so can you.

A PRAYER FOR TODAY

Dear Lord, Thank you for teaching me that seven is Your number; it's the divine number of perfection. And while You gave that number to Joshua and the Israelites for the measure of days until their victory, I know You may have a different number for me. I believe You have a specific and perfect plan for me, and I trust You. Father, please give me the patience not to rush ahead of Your plan. Give me the obedience to follow Your instructions to a tee. No matter the number You have for me, I rejoice because I have faith that a season of joy and triumph is coming for me! I praise You for the victories You have given me in the past, and the victories You are prepared to give me in the future, for I know there is power in praise. In Jesus' name I pray all these things, amen.

EPILOGUE

The journey continues.

I n Joshua chapter 12, we find a list of the kings Joshua and the Israelites defeated during their conquest of Canaan, the promised land. There were thirty-one kings in all. One by one, Israel conquered them all because God was with them. The Lord fought on their behalf.

Likewise, the battle that you are facing today will not be your last. Life truly is a series of hurdles, each designed to make us better, stronger, more faithful, and more Christ-like. When you are faithful, God will continue to fight on your behalf and defeat every obstacle that rises up and stands against you, just as He did for Joshua and the Israelites. He will give you victory time and time again in His way and on His timetable.

Joshua lived to be one hundred and ten years old, and toward the end of his life, he gathered all the tribes of Israel together before the Lord along with the elders, leaders, judges, and officials. Through Joshua, God recounted the history of what He had done for His people, starting with Abraham and taking them through Isaac, Jacob, Moses, and the deliverance out of Egypt. He reminded them of the great and mighty miracles He had performed in the wilderness and how He delivered the Amorites, Perizzites, Canaanites, Hittites, Girgashites, Hivites, and Jebusites into their hands, giving the people the entire land.

Next comes one of my favorite passages of Scripture. Joshua said to the people:

> Now fear the LORD and serve him with all faithfulness. Throw away the gods your ancestors worshiped beyond the Euphrates River and in Egypt, and serve the LORD. But if serving the LORD seems undesirable to you, *then choose for yourselves this day whom you will serve*, whether the gods your ancestors served beyond the Euphrates, or the gods of the Amorites, in whose land you are living. *But as for me and my household, we will serve the LORD.* (Josh. 24:14–15, emphasis added)

Every day, we all have a choice to make. We can choose the gods of our culture—money, fame, power, sex, drugs, alcohol, pride, fashion, technology, self, politics—and worship them. Or we can choose to serve the Lord God Almighty, the Maker of heaven and earth, who has a perfect plan for us.

In his final words to the people of Israel, Joshua declared that, independent of what everyone else chose to do, he and his entire family would continue to serve the Lord. It's the same for us. It doesn't matter what everyone around us is doing, and it makes no difference what or whom everyone else is worshiping. We must decide this day whom we will serve.

As for me and my house, we will serve the Lord. Will you do the same?

AUTHOR'S NOTE

Today, Jericho is a quiet town with a population of about eighteen thousand.[1] Archaeologists have unearthed the layers of more than twenty successive civilizations that date back as early as 9000 BC. It is believed to be one of the oldest continuously inhabited civilizations in the world.[2] It seems that every effort to rebuild the city to its former glory failed miserably after the Israelites' conquest, just as it was foretold in Joshua 6:26.

ACKNOWLEDGMENTS

cknowledgment is a poorly chosen word when fully express-ing one's immense gratitude for a project like this. The very essence of this book is how to achieve the impos-sible when no one gives you a prayer. And the Herculean task of publishing a book doesn't happen unless there is a team of tireless workers who are equally committed and focused to seeing walls fall down, deadlines overcome, and dreams come true.

First and foremost is the Lord God who decided before the creation of the world to give His children the greatest book ever written, the Bible, which is full of stories and truths that help shape our eternal destiny.

Second are my wife and children who sacrifice so much in order to allow me the time that is needed to write that which God has placed on my heart. Until one has tried writing a book, one really does not know how much work and time it requires. Their sacrifice is what enabled this book to become a reality.

Third is Angela Merrill, my writing assistant, who appears to be highly capable of juggling work, pregnancy, and family every time we write a book together. Her newest baby girl, Milani, was born shortly after we turned in the manuscript for *Walls Fall Down*. Angie is more than just a colleague; she is an angel on earth who shares my burden to creatively tell others about God's amazing plan of salvation. Thank you, Angie, for your commitment to the success of this book down to the smallest detail.

Fourth are Andrea and Bryan at Alive Communications who believed in my vision for *Walls Fall Down* from day one, and who championed this book every step of the way. They are truly the best in the business, and I'm so grateful to have their wisdom, support, and encouragement.

Fifth are the wonderful people at Thomas Nelson—Joel, Kristen, Katherine, Julie, Debbie, Ramona, Chad, Stephanie, and Tiffany—who, in the midst of managing other books, still made the time and priority for *Walls Fall Down*. Their level of expertise is off the charts, and I will be forever thankful for their management of this project.

Sixth are all the foot soldiers who have marched in line with me around this book in order for it to become a reality by providing valuable feedback, edits, and suggestions in its initial phases. Carla, Kyle, Elizabeth, Lucille, Jim, Beth, Dennis, and Fawn, thank you for blessing me with the gifts of your time and know-how.

Seventh and last (you didn't think I was going to stop at six did you?) is you, the reader. Your participation in reading and sharing this book creates a wave of momentum that I pray sweeps across our world to let everyone know that with God all things are possible!

NOTES

INTRODUCTION

1. John Noble Wilford, "Believers Score in Battle Over the Battle of Jericho," *New York Times*, February 22, 1990, http://www .nytimes.com/1990/02/22/world/believers-score-in-battle -over-the-battle-of-jericho.html.

DAY 1

1. Numbers 14:7–9.
2. Deuteronomy 31:8.
3. Joshua 1:5–6.
4. Joshua 6:2.
5. John F. Walvoord and Roy B. Zuck, eds., "Destroying Fortresses; Victory at Jericho (Joshua 6:1–27)," *The Bible Knowledge Commentary*, Victor Books, Wheaton, 1983, 1985, available on Bible.org, http://bible.org/seriespage/destroying-fortresses-victory -jericho-joshua-61-27#P741_163114. Emphasis added.
6. The American-Israeli Cooperative Enterprise, "Jericho," Virtual Israel Experience, Jewish Virtual Library, 2012, http://www .jewishvirtuallibrary.org/jsource/vie/Jericho.html.

7. Bryant Wood, "Archaeology Confirms: They Really Did Come A-tumblin' Down," Answersingenesis.org, March 1, 1999, http://www.answersingenesis.org/articles/cm/v21/n2/the-walls-of-jericho.

8. Dan Jackson, "The One and Only God," SermonCentral.com, June 2005, http://www.sermoncentral.com/sermons/the-one-and-only-god-dan-jackson-sermon-on-commandments-no-gods-80935.asp?Page=3.

9. Andrew Moseman, "The Estimated Number of Stars in the Universe Just Tripled," Discover (blog), December 1, 2010, http://blogs.discovermagazine.com/80beats/2010/12/01/the-estimated-number-of-stars-in-the-universe-just-tripled.

10. Carl Zimmer, "How Many Cells Are in Your Body?" National Geographic Phenomena: The Loom, October 23, 2013, http://phenomena.nationalgeographic.com/2013/10/23/how-many-cells-are-in-your-body/.

11. "How Big Really?" BBC Dimensions, http://howbigreally.com/dimension/ancient_worlds/great_wall_of_china.

12. Buff Spies, *Reader's Digest*, November 1991, used in Leland Patrick's sermon "When God Changed His Address." Also found at http://www.sermoncentral.com/illustrations/sermon-illustration-sermon-central-humor-godsomnipotence-70343.asp.

13. Encyclopaedia Britannica Online, s.v. "Jordan River," accessed January 3, 2014, http://www.britannica.com/EBchecked/topic/306217/Jordan-River.

14. John Piper, "The Curse of Careless Worship" (sermon, November 1, 1987, www.DesiringGod.org). ©2013 Desiring God Foundation, www.desiringGod.org.

15. Search results from Biblegateway.com, New International Version, http://www.biblegateway.com/keyword/?search=be%20strong&version1=NIV&searchtype=phrase&resultspp=500.

16. Hudson Taylor, ed., "China for Christ," *China's Millions* 1:1, July, 1875 (London, Morgan & Scott for China Inland Mission, 1875), accessible at http://books.google.com/books/about/China_s_Millions.html?id=7mwQAAAAIAAJ.

17. Sam Storms, *Pleasures Evermore: The Life-Changing Power of Knowing God* (Colorado Springs, CO: Navpress, 2000), 201.

18. S. M. Lockridge, "That's My King," audio recording, Internet Archive, https://archive.org/details/S.M.LockridgePreaching; transcription http://thatsmyking.wordpress.com/words.

19. Michael Mendelson, "Saint Augustine," *The Stanford Encyclopedia of Philosophy* (Winter 2012 Edition), Edward N. Zalta, ed., http://plato.stanford.edu/archives/win2012/entries/augustine.

20. Stephen Seamands, *Ministry in the Image of God: The Trinitarian Shape of Christian Service* (Downers Grove, IL: InterVarsity Press, 2005), 101.

DAY 2

1. Joshua 2:9–13.

2. Joshua 2:14.

3. Joshua 2:16.

4. H. G. Salter, *The Book of Illustrations* (London: J. Hatchard and Son, 1840), 389–90.

5. Robert Zemeckis, director, *Forrest Gump* (Paramount Pictures, 1994).

6. Mike Breaux, "The Heart of Jesus," sermon given at Eastside Christian Church, July 22, 2010, http://vimeo.com/13619210.

7. Search results, BibleGateway, New International Version, accessed January 3, 2014, http://www.biblegateway.com/quicksearch/?quicksearch=trust&qs_version=NIV.

8. Dictionary.com, s.v. "trust," accessed January 3, 2014, http://dictionary.reference.com/browse/trust?s=t&ld=1118.

9. Charles H. Spurgeon, *Psalms,* vol. 2 (Wheaton: Watermark, 1993), 284.

10. Lloyd Ogilvie, *Twelve Steps to Living Without Fear* (Nashville: Thomas Nelson, 1991), 24.

11. John Ortberg, *If You Want to Walk on Water, You've Got to Get Out of the Boat* (Grand Rapids, MI: Zondervan, 2001), 162.

12. William Shakespeare, *Measure for Measure,* act 1, sc. 4, http://shakespeare.mit.edu/measure/measure.1.4.html.

13. BibleStudyTools.com, s.v. "Idiotes," http://www.biblestudytools.com/lexicons/greek/nas/idiotes.html.

14. Congressman J. C. Watts, speech to the GOP National Convention, August 13, 1996, http://www.pbs.org/newshour/bb /politics/july-dec96/watts_08-13.html.
15. Joshua 6:24–25.

DAY 3

1. Bryant G. Wood, "The Walls of Jericho," Associates for Biblical Research, June 9, 2008, http://www.biblearchaeology.org/post /2008/06/the-walls-of-jericho.aspx. Conversion from feet to cubits based on the fact that the retaining wall is said to have been 12 to 15 feet high, the mud-brick walls were said to have been approximately 26 feet high, and 1 cubit equals .677 feet: http:// www.convertunits.com/from/cubits/to/foot.
2. For more on talents and other biblical measurements, see "Weights and Measures," JewishEncyclopedia.com, 1906, http://www .jewishencyclopedia.com/articles/14821-weights-and-measures.
3. Exodus 13:21.
4. Exodus 14:21–28.
5. Exodus 16.
6. Exodus 17:5–6.
7. Jack Hayford, "Jack Hayford Explains What Holiness Really Is," *Charisma* magazine, May 31, 2013, http://www.charismamag .com/spirit/spiritual-growth/14575-wholly-holy.
8. You can follow my son, Dallas, on Instagram @the365movement.
9. This story is taken from a talk Walt Wiley gave during a mission trip in the Dominican Republic in November 2012; also available on the CD from a Winning With Encouragement Ministries seminar, "Standing Out in the Crowd," http://www.wweministries .org/products/standing-out-in-the-crowd.html.
10. Joshua 6:6–7.

DAY 4

1. Numbers 11:1–20.
2. Numbers 14:1–35.
3. Joshua 6:2.
4. Matthew 6:10; Matthew 26:42; John 4:34.

5. Pew Research Center, "Global Christianity—A Report on the Size and Distribution of the World's Christian Population," Pew Research Religion and Public Life Project, December 19, 2011, http://www.pewforum.org/Christian/Global-Christianity-exec.aspx.

6. Keystone Baptist Church, "Why did God confuse the languages of Babel," Pastor's Blog, http://www.keystonebaptist.org/the-news/55-why-did-god-confuse-the-languages-of-babel.html.

7. United States Geographic Society, "Feature Detail Report for: Mount San Antonio," US Department of the Interior, http://geonames.usgs.gov/apex/f?p=gnispq:3:0::NO::P3_FID:273439.

8. Mark Atteberry, *Walking with God on the Road You Never Wanted to Travel* (Nashville: Thomas Nelson, 2005), 33.

9. Michelle Castillo, "Study: Suicide rates among army soldiers up 80 percent," CBS News, July 10, 2012, http://www.cbsnews.com/8301-504763_162-57394452-10391704/study-suicide-rates-among-army-soldiers-up-80-percent.

10. *The International Journal of Missionary Research*, quoted in Southern Baptist Convention, "Persecution," the Ethics and Religious Liberty Commission, http://erlc.com/issues/quick-facts/persecution/.

11. Pat Riley, *The Winner Within: A Life Plan for Team Players* (New York: Berkley, 1994).

DAY 5

1. Numbers 14:1–35.

2. Joshua 5:6–8.

3. According to the Torah, the minimum age for military service is twenty (Numbers 1:3, and Rashi and Nahmanides ad loc.), "Military Law," Jewish Virtual Library, http://www.jewishvirtuallibrary.org/jsource/judaica/ejud_0002_0014_0_13895.html.

4. Numbers 33; Deuteronomy 1:2.

5. Ani, "Half of dieters give up after one month," Yahoo News, November 5, 2012, http://in.news.yahoo.com/half-dieters-one-month-064943950.html.

6. Kimberly Weisul, "84 percent of workers looking to leave their

jobs," CBS Money Watch, December 2 2011, http://www.cbsnews
.com/8301-505125_162-57335303/84-percent-of-workers-looking-to
-leave-their-jobs.

7. Travis Waldron, "Study: Nearly Half of America's College
Students Drop Out Before Receiving a Degree," ThinkProgress
.org, March 28, 2012, http://thinkprogress.org/education/2012/03
/28/453632/half-college-students-drop-out/?mobile=nc.

8. Alan J. Hawkins and Tamara A. Fackrell, *Should I Keep Trying
to Work It Out? A Guidebook for Individuals and Couples at the
Crossroads of Divorce* (Salt Lake City: Utah Commission on
Marriage, 2009), www.divorce.usu.edu/files/uploads/Lesson3.pdf.

9. Susan Ware, ed., *Notable American Women: A Biographical
Dictionary Completing the Twentieth Century* (Cambridge, MA:
Harvard University Press, 2004), 110.

10. Dudley Rutherford, *God Has an App for That!* (Ventura, CA:
Regal, 2012).

11. Sheila Walsh, *Good Morning, Lord* (Nashville: Thomas Nelson,
2010), 128. Also, http://www.bobwieland.com.

12. Dave Ungrady, "25 Years Later, a Marathon Finish Still Inspires,"
New York Times, November 5, 2011, http://www.nytimes.com/2011
/11/06/sports/bob-wielands-athletic-accomplishments-continue
-to-inspire.html?pagewanted=all&_r=2&.

13. "Bob Wieland Walks Across America on His Hands" (video), YouTube,
September 30, 2011, http://www.youtube.com/watch?v=TGPlBgFemx0.

14. Bob Wieland's Team Inspiration, http://www.bobwieland.com/.

15. "Bob Wieland Walks Across America on His Hands," http://www
.youtube.com/watch?v=TGPlBgFemx0.

16. Ibid.

17. Bernie Augustine, "Before Linsanity erupted, Jeremy Lin slept
on NY Knicks teammate Landry Fields' couch," *New York Daily
News*, February 13, 2012, http://www.nydailynews.com/sports
/basketball/knicks/linsanity-erupted-jeremy-lin-slept-ny-knicks
-teammate-landry-fields-couch-article-1.1021809.

18. Eryn Sun, "Jeremy Lin's Favorite Bible Verse Reflects His Story of
Perseverance," *Christian Post Entertainment*, February 18, 2012,
http://m.christianpost.com/news/jeremy-lins-favorite-bible-verse
-reflects-his-story-of-perseverance-69781/.

19. Sun, "Jeremy Lin's Favorite Bible Verse," *Christian Post Entertainment.*

20. Ibid.

21. Malcolm Gladwell, *Outliers* (New York: Little, Brown, 2008), 38–41, 50.

22. Bob Greene, "When Jordan Cried Behind Closed Doors," *Chicago Tribune,* May 15, 1991, http://articles.chicagotribune.com/1991 -05-15/features/9102120922_1_jordan-story-list-basketball-team.

23. Pew Research Center, as quoted in "Fast Food Statistics," Statistic Brain, January 1, 2014, http://www.statisticbrain.com /fast-food-statistics.

24. John C. Maxwell, *Put Your Dream to the Test* (Nashville: Thomas Nelson, 2011), 107.

25. Ben D. Gardner, "Busting the 21 days habit formation myth," Health Behaviour Research Centre Blog, June 29, 2012, http:// blogs.ucl.ac.uk/hbrc/2012/06/29/busting-the-21-days-habit -formation-myth.

DAY 6

1. Source unknown, "Augustine of Hippo Quotes," the European Graduate School, http://www.egs.edu/library/augustine-of-hippo /quotes/.

2. Rick Warren said this at the Resurgence Conference in Seattle, Washington, on November 6, 2013. http://theresurgence.com /pages/r13.

3. Brent Schrotenboer, "Tour de France sees no win in picking another loser," *USA Today,* October 15, 2012, http://www .usatoday.com/story/sports/cycling/2012/10/15/lance-armstrong -tour-de-france-doping/1635499/.

4. Joyce Meyer, *Do It Afraid! Obeying God in the Face of Fear* (New York: Warner Faith, 2003), 19.

5. Steve DuPlessie, *Obeying Jesus: The Seven Commands for Every Disciple* (Attleboro, MA: Anapauo Press, 2011), 4–6.

6. Bible Study Tools, Old Testament Hebrew Lexicon, s.v. "Barak," http://www.biblestudytools.com/lexicons/hebrew/kjv/barak.html.

7. Walter A. Elwell, ed., *Baker's Evangelical Dictionary of Biblical*

Theology, s.v. "Blessedness," BibleStudyTools.com, http://www
.biblestudytools.com/dictionaries/bakers-evangelical-dictionary
/blessedness.html.

8. Oswald Chambers, *So I Send You: A Series of Missionary Studies* (London: Simpkin Marshall, 1930), 47.

9. "The Obstinate Lighthouse," Snopes, January 3, 2014, http://
www.snopes.com/military/lighthouse.asp.

DAY 7

1. Joshua 6:4–5.

2. Joshua 6:16–17.

3. Matthew George Easton, *Easton's Bible Dictionary*, s.v. "Seven," BibleStudyTools.com, http://www.biblestudytools.com/dictionaries /eastons-bible-dictionary/seven.html; R. L. Harris, Gleason L. Archer, and Bruce K. Waltke, *Theological Wordbook of the Old Testament* (Chicago: Moody Press, 1980), 898.

4. The word *seven* appears 338 times in the NIV version of the Bible, and the word *seventh* appears 119 times. Search results, Bible Gateway, New International Version, http://www.biblegateway.com /keyword/?search=seven&version1=31&searchtype=all&wholewor dsonly=yes&resultspp=500; http://www.biblegateway.com/kcywor d/?search=seventh&version1=31&searchtype=all&wholewordsonly =yes&resultspp=500.

5. Encyclopedia Britannica Online, s.v. "Laura Ingalls Wilder," http://www.britannica.com/EBchecked/topic/643657/Laura -Ingalls-Wilder.

6. Encyclopedia Britannica Online, s.v. "Ronald W. Reagan," http:// www.britannica.com/EBchecked/topic/492882/Ronald-W-Reagan.

7. Michael Body, "David Seidler, a writer who found his voice," *The Australian,* March 7, 2011, http://www.theaustralian.com.au/news /features/david-seidler-a-writer-who-found-his-voice/story-e6frg6z6 -1226016762328.

8. "Louis Zamperini," Memorie Shop, http://www.memorieshop.com /Cinema/Unbroken/index.html.

9. "Louis Zamperini," Concordia University Irvine, http://www.cui .edu/giving/gala/index.aspx?id=22288.

10. Janet Chismar, "Louis Zamperini's Story of Survival and Redemption," Billy Graham Evangelistic Association, May 27, 2011, http://www.billygraham.org/articlepage.asp?articleid=7916.
11. Brett Johnson, "Louis Zamperini lives to talk about horrific plane crash, 47 days lost at sea and POW camp," *Ventura County Star*, April 13, 2013, http://www.vcstar.com/news/2013/apr/13/louis -zamperini-lives-to-talk-about-horrific-47.
12. George Müller, *Autobiography of George Müller: A Million and a Half in Answer to Prayer* (Vestavia Hills, AL: Solid Ground Christian Books, 2004), 693.
13. "George Mueller, Orphanages Built by Prayer," Christianity.com, http://www.christianity.com/church/church-history/church-history -for-kids/george-mueller-orphanages-built-by-prayer-11634869.html.
14. Matthew 24:31; 1 Corinthians 15:52; 1 Thessalonians 4:16.
15. Joshua 6:22.
16. Joshua 6:27.

AUTHOR'S NOTE

1. Applied Research Institute—Jerusalem, "Jericho," 2008, page 12, http://vprofile.arij.org/jericho/vdata.php.
2. The American-Israeli Cooperative Enterprise, "Jericho," Virtual Israel Experience, 2012, http://www.jewishvirtuallibrary.org/jsource /vie/Jericho.html.

ABOUT THE AUTHOR

D udley Rutherford is the senior pastor of the 10,000-member Shepherd Church, which the mayor of Los Angeles has called "the most racially diverse church in Los Angeles." Dudley and his wife, Renee, and their three children reside in Northridge, California. His other published works are *God Has an App for That*, *Unleashed: The Church Turning the World Upside Down*, *Romancing Royalty*, and *Proverbs in a Haystack*.

PRAISE FOR *WALLS FALL DOWN*

I can be moved by a message and I can be inspired by a messenger, but once in a while a message and a messenger come together in such a way that the impact is transforming. Dudley Rutherford is God's messenger for this message. I have followed him a number of times over the years as God has used him to lead the march around the walls. With a great balance of information and inspiration Dudley will challenge you to face whatever walls you're up against with the power of God.

—KYLE IDLEMAN, TEACHING PASTOR, SOUTHEAST
CHRISTIAN CHURCH, AND AUTHOR OF *NOT A FAN*

Walls Fall Down is an epic book about an epic battle with an epic victory.

—MANNY PACQUIAO, WORLD CHAMPION PROFESSIONAL BOXER

Dudley Rutherford is a modern-day Joshua—courageous, strong, immersed in the Word and unafraid to face the battle ahead if he knows he is on God's side. If you have a battle looming in your life, Dudley explains how to draw on the truth and power of God to tear that wall down. A must read for all looking for victory in their lives.

—RANDY FRAZEE, SENIOR MINISTER, OAK HILLS CHURCH, AND
AUTHOR OF *THE HEART OF THE STORY* AND *THINK, ACT, BE LIKE JESUS*

I know of no other man who could write about how God removes walls more than Dudley Rutherford. His life and ministry live out the truth of God's supernatural power. I am very excited about how God is going to use this book around the globe. Read it and share it with the world!

—DR. RONNIE FLOYD, SENIOR PASTOR, CROSS CHURCH,
AND AUTHOR OF *THE POWER OF PRAYER AND FASTING*

In *Walls Fall Down*, Dudley Rutherford combines penetrating Biblical insight with loads of personal experience to help us face the walls in our own lives. I loved Dudley's depth and practicality and found so much that I could use in my own life. This is a life-giving resource, written with great care, to help you face any problem you are up against.

—JUD WILHITE, SENIOR PASTOR, CENTRAL CHRISTIAN
CHURCH, AND AUTHOR OF *THE GOD OF YES*

This book has such a powerful message that has the potential to change many lives. In *Walls Fall Down*, Dudley Rutherford presents the challenges we all face in a new light, a blessed assurance that we serve the same God today who delivered the Israelites so long ago. Walking in the calling we have on our lives is possible, but we must practice consistency and surround ourselves with those who will challenge us and lift us up. Life is supposed to be taken one day at a time, and this book will help unlock the secrets of living a fulfilled life and achieving great victory. There are times when everybody feels like giving up, but if we train our minds to see the glory of God in all things, we will step into a life of unimaginable blessing and untold potential. The same God who parted the seas raised the dead lives within us, and He has an amazing future waiting for us if we would only have faith; big things are only achieved through big prayers and an unshakeable resolve.

—MATTHEW BARNETT, SENIOR PASTOR, ANGELUS TEMPLE,
AND CO-FOUNDER OF THE DREAM CENTER

Walls Fall Down is a terrific new book. I can't wait for you to read it and put these truths into action.

—PAT WILLIAMS, SENIOR VICE PRESIDENT, ORLANDO MAGIC,
AND AUTHOR OF *COACH WOODEN'S GREATEST SECRET*

Dudley Rutherford characterizes a rising generation of church leaders who touch the hearts of multitudes because they live with a heart of pure passion for God, His Word, and His People. I readily affirm the value of his message and ministry and believe you will be enriched by his latest book, *Walls Fall Down*.

—DR. JACK W. HAYFORD, CHANCELLOR, THE KING'S
UNIVERSITY, DALLAS AND LOS ANGELES

Walls Fall Down is a fascinating book of perspective that is sure to evoke a swelling sense of hope, perseverance, patience, and trust in God! Pastor Dudley has done an amazing job of taking a commonly referenced Bible-experience and presenting applicable and relative steps for conquering any giant and tearing down even the most seemingly impenetrable walls!

—MARK JACKSON, NBA HALL OF FAMER

Everyone has a unique "Jericho moment" in our lives when we face a seemingly insurmountable wall. Not me. Not anymore. After reading Dudley Rutherford's fascinating book *Walls Fall Down*, I now have a battle plan for what seems impossible. I've marked up my copy and I'm leaving it on my desk. Thanks to this book, the next time I face an obstacle—I have the answer.

—PHIL COOKE, FILMMAKER, MEDIA CONSULTANT, AND AUTHOR
OF *ONE BIG THING: DISCOVERING WHAT YOU WERE BORN TO DO*

Dudley Rutherford is a rare jewel. He "gets it." When he speaks, we all ought to listen. When he writes, we all ought to read. Why? Because he has answers to the really tough questions—questions about how to make life work. It is not by accident that more than 10,000 people gather to hear him each weekend. They are hungry for truth, and for an authentic life behind that truth. If I was not a pastor myself and lived anywhere near his church, I would be sitting close to the front every week, drinking it in. But I can't. Perhaps you can't either. But you can get this book and read it. Do it.

—DR. JIM GARLOW, SENIOR PASTOR, SKYLINE CHURCH,
AND *NEW YORK TIMES* BEST-SELLING AUTHOR

As you are staring at your wall, remember God is staring at you—ready to give you His battle plan. Each day a chapter, each chapter a strategy, and each spiritual strategy a day closer to your walk to victory. Come on. Take the seven-day challenge. It's not where your heels have been but where your toes are pointed. Don't just walk around your wall. Walk through it. Your wall is getting ready to come down. Get ready for a season of joy!

—KEN WHITTEN, PASTOR, EXCITING IDLEWILD BAPTIST CHURCH

Far too many books claim they will help you win the battles in your life. What makes *Walls Fall* Down unique is Dudley Rutherford gives you the actual battle plan and allows you to see the victory that is ahead. He weaves narrative and historical account exquisitely and mixes in modern day application as he sets the stage to make triumph possible in your life. Dudley has a way of communicating that is profound, yet accessible. If you or someone you know are currently in a battle or sense one may be looming (don't we all?), you have to get this book!

—JEFF VINES, LEAD PASTOR, CHRIST'S CHURCH OF THE VALLEY

Each and every one of us are guaranteed to have trials and tribulations in this life. And each and every one of us, at one time or another, try to address and deal with those challenges on our own accord. In his new book entitled *Walls Fall Down*, Pastor Dudley Rutherford shares God's plan as to how we can truly work through, be better for, and face life's adversity, ultimately for God's glory. I am blessed to call Dudley my pastor and dear friend.

—FRANK SONTAG, HOST OF THE *FRANK SONTAG SHOW* ON 99.5 KKLA

Dudley Rutherford takes you on a journey to Jericho as only he can. He walks you through scripture, captivates you with stories, and gives you the courage to face your obstacles in the strength of the Lord. Follow these seven principles and the walls in your life will come a tumblin' down.

—DAVE STONE, SENIOR PASTOR, SOUTHEAST CHRISTIAN CHURCH

No one is immune to the inevitable battles in life, but God is passionate about His people living in joy and victory. That's why my friend Dudley Rutherford has written this wonderful book called *Walls Fall Down*. By unearthing seven secrets from the battle of Jericho in the Bible, Dudley shares clear steps to help each of us overcome whatever challenge we might be facing today. Read *Walls Fall Down* and discover God's great secrets to success.

—MILES MCPHERSON, FORMER NFL PLAYER, SENIOR PASTOR, THE ROCK CHURCH, AND AUTHOR OF *GOD IN THE MIRROR*

The story of Joshua and the walls of Jericho is a dramatic story in which God reveals His power and shows that He delivers on His promises. In his book *Walls Fall Down*, Pastor Dudley Rutherford inspires us to believe God and obey His guidance so that the walls that keep us personally from accomplishing what God has clearly led us to do will collapse. This book will ignite a powerful blend of faith, courage, and trust in your life as a believer. I recommend this book to anyone who desires to see the walls of opposition crumble and God to reveal himself in our greatest battles.

—PHILIP WAGNER, PASTOR, OASIS CHURCH, AND AUTHOR OF *THE MARRIAGE MAKEOVER* AND *LOVE WORKS*